THE SACRED FIRE

THE SACRED FIRE

Love as a Spiritual Path

HENRY JAMES BORYS

HarperSanFrancisco
A Division of HarperCollins*Publishers*

*The stories in this book are based
on the experiences of actual people, but the
names and circumstances have been altered
to ensure confidentiality.*

For information about speaking engagements
and seminars by Henry J. Borys, please write
12756 103rd Place NE, Kirkland, WA 98034.

Book Design by Ralph Fowler
Set in Guardi

FIRST EDITION

Library of Congress Cataloging-in-Publication Data:

Borys, Henry James.
   The sacred fire : love as a spiritual path / Henry James
Borys. —1st ed.
      p.   cm.
   ISBN 0–06–250273–5 (pbk. : acid-free paper)
   1. Marriage.   2. Love.   3. Intimacy (Psychology)
4. Interpersonal relations.   I. Title
HQ734.B7411   1994
306.7—dc20   93–48113
                                                      CIP

94 95 96 97 98 ❖ CWI 10 9 8 7 6 5 4 3 2 1

*To the Divine, and to
all lovers of God, by whose light we are
learning of Love.*

CONTENTS

ACKNOWLEDGMENTS

Though I have written the words in this book, it is what others have given to me that has brought *The Sacred Fire* to life. My deepest gratitude to:

Susan, my wife; I know of no one more purely committed to the path of love. Behind each page lies her immeasurable giving.

Our daughters, Gemma and Sudha, for the inexpressible delight their spirits have awakened in my heart.

Our parents, who gave us our most important first lessons in love, and whose example inspired the desire and courage to walk this path.

The many clients and friends who have allowed me to share in their love and their trials.

John Loudon, Executive Editor, and all the staff at Harper San Francisco, without whose imagination and talent this book would never have materialized.

Judy Delaney, whose appreciation and enthusiasm first sparked *The Sacred Fire*.

THE PROMISE
OF THE HEART

*D*eep within the human heart lies a promise: Life can be incomparably happier, deeper, and richer when we share it with someone we love. Within the intimate companionship of a love relationship, we have the opportunity to experience the highest within ourselves, the highest within life. Here we can open to the most significant personal growth we will experience in our lifetimes.

Nearly every day I counsel couples who have felt the truth of this promise. Like millions of others, they have felt it deeply enough to commit to a lifelong relationship. Yet by the time these couples seek help, their relationship has become a tangled mess of reaction, resentment, and bitterness, of confusion and disappointment—of misery, not happiness. It is no secret that half of all marriages in this country end in divorce; how many more couples, married and unmarried, feel dissatisfied with their relationships? Considering all the casualties it claims, the quest for living the promise of the heart might as well be for the Holy Grail.

Yet the impulse of our hearts toward intimacy is not wrong. There *is* great truth within this promise, but living that truth is far more demanding than the simplicity and beauty of the promise of the heart suggests.

Put any two people intimately together, each with his or her own backgrounds, expectations, desires, and quirks, and you're bound to get a few surprises. As the nineteenth-century American statesman John Hay gibed, "Maidens! Why should you worry in choosing whom you shall marry? Choose whom you may, you will find you have gotten somebody else." The person you thought to be sensitive and intelligent may leave dirty socks strewn around the living room. The partner you knew to be tender and appreciative may eventually critique you with a cutting edge sharper than Siskel and Ebert brandish on the latest bad movie.

The problems that arise in an intimate relationship, however, are not merely roadblocks. Here, as in every sphere of life, they serve a purpose. As Scott Peck points out in *The Road Less Traveled,*

> *Problems call forth our courage and our wisdom; indeed, they create our courage and our wisdom. It is only because of problems that we grow mentally and spiritually. When we desire to encourage the growth of the human spirit, we challenge and encourage the human*

The Promise of the Heart

capacity to solve problems, just as in school we deliber-
ately set problems for our children to solve. It is through
the pain of confronting and resolving problems that we
learn.

In this book we will learn how the challenges we experience in an intimate relationship—the conflicts, resentments, hurts, and disappointments, and even the periods of alienation, boredom, and absence of affection—are not unfortunate and meaningless obstacles to our happiness. On the contrary, they are profoundly meaningful. They arise precisely where we are still developing in our ability to love—where we may be attached, insensitive, unfeeling, self-centered, or blind to ourselves. They arise to open our hearts, to open our eyes, to balance us, to free us to love fully and unconditionally.

Even more important, we will learn that this growth need not be a trial by fire. As we open to discovering the meaning of our challenges together, we begin to live the joys of love much more deeply and consistently. The fire of intimacy grows brighter, but also softer. Instead of searing with its heat, it casts a hallowed light, revealing all that is most human and sacred within us, as it guides our way on the path of love.

CHAPTER ONE

ON THE PATH OF LOVE

Opening to Personal Meaning

As most of us find out sooner or later, the path of love is nothing if not challenging. It offers some of life's most breathtaking views and richest rewards, but takes unexpected twists and turns. It forces us to squeeze through narrow passages and to climb rugged peaks. Yet, with all this, love is a path that we can travel joyfully.

I developed a passion for exploring the intricacies of love as a path because of the ways my own marriage has challenged me to grow. I am more than simply grateful for this growth: The richness it has brought to my life is inestimable. The thought of what my life might have been otherwise—the limitations in awareness, in attitudes, in my ability to give, to love, to experience life—reminds me of the supreme preciousness of my relationship with my wife, Susan. (To say nothing of the countless joys we have shared through our love.)

At the beginning of our marriage, for instance, I saw myself as virtually above most household tasks. Coming home after a long day of work and having to help clean the house, do the laundry, or wash the dishes seemed out of the question. I felt that I deserved to relax. I directed my energy and commitment to my career, not to mundane household details. Somehow these would get taken care of (my wife would do them). I thought I was as loving as the next husband, when, in this respect at least, I was actually a young wife's nightmare.

As a result of this attitude, my "lack of giving" soon became a major problem in our relationship. This issue sparked arguments almost every week. Looking back, I can see how easy it would have been to simply pitch in. In truth, however, my challenge went deeper than merely lending a hand around the house. My wife needed more than my grudging participation. She needed my caring, support, and nurturing, a true sense of intimacy and loving companionship. In a word, she needed my love.

Learning to love means developing genuine sensitivity to each other's needs—caring, compassion, understanding, and selflessness. My lack of participation around the house was a symptom of my limited ability to love. My attitude and the resulting conflicts thus held a profound message for me. Unfortunately, I was not yet ready to understand this.

This problem within our relationship was not to be solved simply by divvying up household tasks. In fact, we did sometimes manage to split up specific household tasks, and I held up my end quite well (out of sheer stubbornness). Still, my newfound ability to do housework hardly transformed our relationship—or me. It was not until my marriage was threatened—by my wife's deep romantic friendship with another man—that I was motivated to look within and face how I had failed to nurture her. That situation became a major turning point in the course of our relationship, and opened me to discovering a whole new level of my ability to love.*

THE CHALLENGE OF INTIMACY: DISCOVERING PERSONAL MEANING

E very challenge we run up against on the path of love presents us with the opportunity to discover our *personal meaning* in the situation: the way in which we can use this challenge to grow and deepen as human beings. The first thing most of us do in times of conflict is to find fault with the other person. Eventually, however, we need to stop blaming our partner and ask ourselves honestly, Why does this problem arise again and again? What is this situation evoking in me? How is it challenging me to grow, to become stronger, more creative, more loving?

Such inward reflections spark our journey of growth through our relationship. Discovering personal meaning,

*I relate the details of this turning point in our marriage in a previous book, *The Way of Marriage: A Journal of Spiritual Growth Through Conflict, Love, and Sex* (San Francisco: HarperSanFrancisco, 1993).

however, is not simply an intellectual process of self-analysis. As we shall see, actual growth involves an opening and a shift within our whole being—within our mind, our heart, and even our body; only then do we fully discover personal meaning, in the moment of our transformation. As psychologist Carl Jung observed, "No one develops his personality because somebody tells him that it would be useful or advisable to do so. Nature has never yet been taken in by well-meaning advice. The only thing that moves nature is causal necessity, and that goes for human nature too. Without necessity nothing budges, the human personality least of all . . . The developing personality obeys no caprice, no command, no insight, only brute necessity; it needs the motivating force of inner or outer fatalities." To grow through the problems we encounter together, we must open ourselves to feeling this personal necessity.

Most of us, however, enter intimate relationships innocently, with no idea of what we are letting ourselves in for. We fail to recognize that we are fledglings in love, that for the most part, our love is motivated by our desire for personal happiness. We hope we will find happiness through the joys of companionship, through sexual fulfillment, through the security of a relationship, and perhaps through having children. Thus we actually love *ourselves,* our own desires, through each other. We may have only the barest glimpse of what it means to truly love each other.

On the Path of Love

This is not to belittle what we feel. Whether in the fresh bloom of romance or in a mature relationship, our feelings are a spontaneous experience. They are a part of life's process, and therefore a part of life's truth. Our hope for happiness through each other is also natural and healthy. It initiates our involvement in the relationship. It sets us on the path of love. If there is an element of illusion in romance, fine. Love's illusions can bring us to the door of love's truth. Our attachments can become the path to our freedom. Our unconscious motivations can set us on this path to expanding our awareness. Our self-serving love can sow the seeds of selfless love and giving. Again, in order for this to happen, however, we must consciously recognize our need to grow.

Yet even with an intention to do so, trying to open to love's challenges may seem frustrating. We may find it far easier to meet the challenges of our lives in other areas—in school, sports, politics, business. The reason for this is the deeply personal nature of love's challenges: Intimacy tests not merely what we know, or what we can do, but our most personal, human qualities: How much do we care? How much do we give? How deeply and innocently do we feel? How open are we? How selflessly do we love? The challenges of love penetrate to the very heart of our being—to where they must open and heal our hearts. But because they are so personal, we can miss these challenges of the heart altogether.

For instance, unlike me, a good friend of mine was exemplary—as far as participating around the house was concerned. Without being asked, he tended to their children, took care of most of the housecleaning, insisted on single-handedly cleaning up after every meal (many of which he cooked), and frequently undertook creative projects to reorganize the house more efficiently. In addition, he ran his own very successful business; he was an excellent provider. Whenever I visited his home, I sat in amazement as I watched what seemed to me the living embodiment of the perfect husband and father.

One evening, as he was busy washing the dishes, I commented to his wife how lucky she was to have such a husband. To my surprise, she made a face and launched into a barrage of complaints. According to her, he kept their house *too* clean and tidy. She said it drove her crazy to always have everything in its place and sparkling clean. At the time, this struck me as the most unwarranted negativity on her part. Indeed, it made me admire my friend even more; in addition to his other virtues, he possessed unfathomable patience with a hypercritical wife. The man was a modern saint.

As I later learned, however, her aggravation related to a much deeper complaint. Her husband had great difficulty in communicating and especially in showing his feelings. This contributed to tremendous alienation between him and his wife. Over their years together, she had grown to feel alone, insecure, and isolated.

On the Path of Love

A couple of years later, the problems between them peaked. On the verge of divorce, they sought counseling. Gradually, he opened to the deep emotional wounds that had driven him to distance himself from his feelings, and began to heal. This marked a tremendous personal awakening, and he and his wife experienced a deep renewal of their closeness and appreciation for each other.

I had known this man for years. We had shared a deep friendship, and he had never distanced himself from me. It took the unique intimacy of a long-term love relationship to challenge him to make a deeper, more personal connection with his own feelings. His marriage provided him with a unique and powerful opportunity to deepen and heal himself, and he took it.

Unfortunately, many couples, failing to actualize this power of an intimate relationship to heal and vitalize their lives, experience a loss of energy. Over time, they gradually lose interest in each other as the enthusiasm with which they once shared interests and activities ebbs.

Many people blame this phenomenon on practical concerns, such as careers, kids, bills, laundry, and yard work. By themselves, however, these cannot cause us to slip into a routine of nonenergetic relating. Busy people find time to fall in love, and many individuals languishing in lackluster relationships miraculously muster the energy to have impassioned affairs.

The problem is more basic than not having enough time or energy. When we fail to meet and grow through life's challenges, we lose something essential to our lives. We lose life. For example, the child who fails to pay attention in school gets bored; the would-be athlete who neglects practice soon gets discouraged and quits; the employee who works halfheartedly accomplishes little and usually complains a lot. This also applies to love. When we fail to open our hearts to the profound personal meaning of our lives together, the life of our relationship will gradually ebb.

OPENING TO PERSONAL MEANING

*O*pening to personal meaning is the first secret of living the promise of the heart. But to do this, we must see our relationship as a path of growth. For example, if my partner consistently refuses to have sex with me, and I see our relationship only as a vehicle for bringing me happiness on my own terms, then I may argue, badger, plead, or barter to get my way. If these methods fail, I may have an affair or end the relationship. If I see my relationship as a path of growth, however, I may become open to an entirely different significance. I may, for instance, discover that my mate's refusal relates to my own failure to nurture my partner outside of the bedroom; I may realize how this challenge in our relationship is perfectly suited to deepening me and my ability to love more maturely. In opening myself to this discovery, I am already deepening. I am transcending that universal limitation to love that says, "I already know; I already am capable of love, I deserve to have things my way, our problems must be your fault."

Every persistent problem in a relationship involves both partners. When two join together in an intimate relationship, a complex chemistry of feeling is created, one which envelopes us and within which we think, feel, react, and interact. This complex chemistry draws upon the strength of our love, awareness, sensitivity, and giving. It also highlights our personal blind spots, attachments, and imbalances. Thus, a relationship holds innumerable challenges to grow, and the subtle chemistry of intimacy is an unlimited storehouse of personal meaning—layer upon layer of meaning relating to the development of the full potential of our personality, our wisdom, and our ability to love.

The first key to unlocking the treasures of this storehouse is our intention and commitment to unlocking it. Only when we really commit ourselves to something do we enter a relationship with life that yields meaning and growth. In response to our intention, life lets us know how we must grow and exert ourselves in order to achieve our desires.

The moment I commit to excel at tennis, for instance, I begin to activate a sphere of personal meaning. If I have a weak forehand, don't practice, or am a sore loser, I will receive feedback—from my body, my score, or my tennis partner—prodding me to learn, grow, and develop the specific skill, knowledge, and qualities of character necessary to realize my goal. Notice that I am speaking in terms of an intention to excel. Little commitment will yield little result. If I only want to dabble at tennis, many subtleties of the game—as well as many subtle challenges to develop my character—will escape me.

The same holds true of our aspiration to live the joys of an intimate love relationship. A casual interest in love will yield little growth. A commitment to perfect ourselves in love opens the door to all the subtleties of personal meaning relating to love. As Erich Fromm points out in *The Art of Loving*, "The mastery of the art must be a matter of ultimate concern; there must be nothing else in the world more important than the art. This holds true for music, for medicine, for carpentry—and for love." In regard to mastering the art of loving, St. Teresa of Avila goes even farther:

> *They must have a great and very resolute determination to persevere until reaching the end, come what may, happen what may, whatever work is involved, whatever criticism arises, whether they arrive or whether they die on the road, or even if they don't have courage for the trials that are met, or if the whole world collapses.*

STANDING IN THE UNKNOWN

As vital as intention and commitment are, however, these are not everything. We cannot simply manufacture personal meaning at will. I may tell myself that all of the challenges in my relationship are for my growth, but this is merely an idea. I may still react to my partner's shortcomings as much as ever. Likewise, after giving it some thought, I may conclude that my partner's unwillingness to have sex with me means that I need to become more loving outside of the bedroom. If I have not deeply felt the truth of this, however, then it is still just an idea that aspires to personal meaning. It has not yet arrived.

We *discover* true personal meaning, we do not manufacture it. Our beliefs, intentions, and commitment only open a door to that discovery. True personal meaning emerges from the unknown: from the depths of life, from the depths of our own unconscious, from the frontiers of our growth. It is so transformative because it is alive.

Early in my counseling career, I experienced a surprising example of how unpredictable and mysterious personal meaning can be. John and Candace, an unmarried couple, came to see me because they felt their relationship was about to end. As usual, I began the first counseling session by asking each partner what he or she hoped to gain from counseling.

Candace, an articulate woman, gave a striking answer. She spoke about how she wanted to establish a strong commitment to work at their relationship. She wanted them to focus on being together, on communicating, on giving to each other, so that they would not drift apart or feel numb in their relationship. In short, she wanted to use their relationship for growth. She continued in this vein quite eloquently for several minutes, beautifully articulating my own philosophy of what is possible within a relationship. I was impressed.

Then I turned to John. John seemed much younger than Candace, and was somewhat shy and withdrawn. In a few words, he affirmed that he wanted the same things as Candace, and lapsed into a self-conscious silence. Admittedly, Candace was a hard act to follow.

As the session continued, their story unfolded. John and Candace had been together for eight years. Candace was now in her early forties, and John was only twenty-seven. He had never experienced another intimate relationship in his life. As much as he did feel love for Candace, John was also feeling an irrepressible desire to be on his own, to experience what life might hold for him. John could not help wondering what he might miss by continuing in his relationship with Candace. He had been fighting this urge for freedom for several years, and now felt that he could fight it no longer. As much as I agreed with Candace's goals for their relationship, I could clearly sense an innocence within John's confusion.

Candace felt that John's feelings were something they should work through within the relationship. She believed they should be able to talk through and deal with John's desire for freedom, just as with any issue that arises in a committed relationship. This sounded good, but the more Candace talked, the more I sensed a hidden desperation to not lose the man she loved.

When I asked John if he also wanted to work through his desire for freedom within the relationship, he said he didn't think that he could. He added that the more Candace pressed him for commitment, the more clearly he knew that he needed to get away.

At this point, Candace revealed the extent of her desperation to hold on to John. She suggested that they get married, and then, within that commitment, she would be willing to give John complete freedom to leave her and discover whatever he needed. To this John remained silent.

Certainly, there were issues and challenges for John to address within himself that might have led to a strengthening of their relationship. Yet it seemed clear that the first step was for Candace to ease off; to give John space. How else could John even feel his love for her? How else could he even want to work through anything? Her desperation was only accentuating his desire for freedom.

Candace's desire to grow through their relationship was fine, but all her efforts to do so "together"—through working on their relationship, communicating, and so on—were an expression of the problem, not the solution.

Candace needed to let go. She had to use this challenge in their relationship to rediscover herself, not their relationship, as her center. She was being challenged to heal the hidden sources of her need, and so find her own strength to love without clinging. There was no way to know if this would save their relationship, but clearly it was a necessary step, and probably the best hope of rekindling John's love.

Since that day, in my work with other couples and in my own marriage, I have discovered that when we rise to meet our individual challenges to grow, we are inevitably acting in the best interests of the relationship as well (though this does not always guarantee that the relationship will survive). Few situations make this so clear as when one partner is emotionally dependent on the other. Time and again, relationships are nearly destroyed by the consequences of clinging, only to become revitalized when individuals can heal the underlying sources of their emotional dependency.

No one can tell us what the personal meaning of a situation is for us. Even though I saw a direction of growth for Candace in her situation, for example, even if I clearly analyzed and explained it to her, this would not constitute personal meaning for her. Nor could she find personal meaning by figuring it out intellectually. It must be deeper than that.

This is the essence of personal meaning: simply, innocently *feeling* the significance within our challenges, in a state of openness and surrender, while standing in the unknown. The English poet John Keats described this as "negative capability"—the ability to remain "in uncertainties, mysteries, doubts, without any irritable reaching after fact and reason." Keats considered this an essential quality of greatness, and so do I, for it allows us to be molded and healed by the evolutionary power within life. It allows us to grow, to become the creative, loving personalities we can be.

Thus, contrary to popular belief, analyzing our problems intellectually can sometimes be a great obstacle to personal growth. I have met many couples, vitally interested in personal growth, who could perfectly articulate their own (and their partner's) challenges to grow. Yet their relationships were still stuck; in many cases, their analysis of themselves and each other had become destructive. When we work only through the intellect, we too easily remain encapsulated from life. Caught in our ideas, we miss the experience, which can mold and deepen us.

Perhaps this is why the greatest growth usually comes when we feel challenged nearly to the breaking point. In crisis, our intellectual barriers are breached, and we may finally feel a sense of surrender. We may at last allow ourselves to understand that our lives are far too complex to yield entirely to our conscious control. It is at this point of innocent surrender that we cease to blame each other, cease to cling to others. We empty ourselves, open ourselves to the unknown, and allow life to guide us.

Fortunately, Candace eventually did reach this point of surrender. Through continued one-on-one counseling

(John declined to participate beyond our first session, as he felt certain he needed to leave the relationship), Candace revealed her deep-rooted fears of abandonment. As she allowed herself to feel the pain she was avoiding by holding onto John, she began to realize that rather than try to "fix" this relationship, she could allow its reality to help her to come to terms with and heal those fears. In opening to her fears, she began to use her relationship for her growth and healing—even as it seemed on the verge of ending.

As Candace opened to, released, and healed that pain, she began to feel stronger within herself. A breakthrough came in our final session, when she said that if John did decide to leave, she knew that she would not experience the devastation she had once feared. She knew she would be okay; life would go on. She had discovered a new level of dignity within herself and trust in life.

Once we do open our hearts to a deeper level of meaning, a sense of peace and grace often begins to replace the previous sense of frustration associated with problems. Candace came to feel this sense of peace and grace within herself, and it allowed her to let go of John. I am not sure what became of their relationship, but at least Candace used her challenge to deepen her relationship with herself, and so became more capable of giving and receiving love.

As Candace discovered, true personal meaning always transcends our relationship with others. It comes from our innermost relationship with ourselves and with life. This means that we need not depend on crises to throw us into growth. Personal meaning is always there, in the core of our feelings. The art of living requires our remaining open to it, whether the challenges we face are great or small.

When we remain open in this way, we directly experience the sacredness of life. What is this life that is outside of our control, that seems to lead us in ways that we cannot intellectually anticipate, or even appreciate at the time? What is this life that challenges us to heal ourselves, to become more whole, loving, and fulfilled? To *consciously* open ourselves to what each situation offers is to feel a deeply personal relationship with a beneficent source of meaning beyond our ego, will, and intellect. Within this, we experience the preciousness of our lives together. This path that is our relationship becomes a journey into grace.

CHAPTER TWO

THE ART OF RECEIVING

Learning to Love Unconditionally

As important as personal meaning is to the life of a relationship, there is something even more essential: love.

Love is impossible to define precisely. It entails attraction, affection, tenderness, caring, sensitivity, compassion, understanding, nurturing, selflessness, and many more qualities. What love is could easily become the subject of a book in itself. Yet when we speak of love in the context of an intimate relationship, there is one element key to our *experience* of love: namely, a generous, unconditional appreciation of each other's uniqueness and beauty.

When we deeply appreciate each other, we feel our love, and we feel spontaneously drawn toward each other. In those moments of deep appreciation, we naturally want to nurture, care for, and give to one another. In short, when we feel deeply appreciative of another's beauty, most if not all of the essential aspects of love follow naturally.

When we do not appreciate each other for some reason—say, following an argument—we may "know" we love each other, but in that moment we cannot feel it. We may do our best to act sensitively, attempt to nurture, try to give selflessly; but so long as we do not feel love, well, then we are not feeling love. There is a world of difference between grudgingly spending an evening with my wife because I know I should, and spending an evening with her when I feel drawn by love. I am reminded of Robert Frost's comment, "Pressed into service means pressed out of shape." No matter how good our intentions, attempting to act as if we feel love when in fact we do not feel it is weakening—to ourselves and to the relationship. We will not experience the joy of loving, and our partner will be deprived of the joy of being loved. If this behavior continues, resentment and alienation may build. We may lose the life of the relationship, despite our best intentions.

Treading the path of love without feeling love is a dry, uphill battle. We are sure to exhaust ourselves long before we gain even a glimpse the promise of the heart. Thus we cannot leave the feeling of love to chance. Learning to cultivate our love *is* the path of love.

One way to cultivate our love is to consciously nurture a generous, unconditional appreciation of each other's uniqueness and beauty. I call this the art of receiving.

What we appreciate, we automatically receive; we take it into ourselves, and it expands our experience of life. We do not have to work to receive, nor do we have to add anything: We simply have to be open to receiving what is already there, what is highest in each other. Through our appreciation for another, we receive the gift of that person, and the gift of our own experience of love.

RECEIVING WHAT IS ALREADY THERE

*M*y grandfather gave me my first great experience of the art of receiving. Whenever my sisters, brother, and I were with our grandfather, he thoroughly entered our world. He seemed to possess an endless capacity to delight in our childhood innocence and play. Not once do I remember his delight in us fading. Not once do I remember him distracted, inattentive, or favoring the company of adults or a football game on TV over us. He fully appreciated us, he appreciated the *best* in us, and we felt loved beyond measure. Even to this day I can hardly comprehend the fullness of love I received from my grandfather. I am further amazed when I think that he gave this love despite severe pain from a disabling illness. Years later, I learned that many people recognized his unique gift for receiving not only his grandchildren, but adults as well.

Anyone who has ever felt thoroughly received— through the unconditional love of a parent or best friend, for example—knows that it is one of life's highest experiences. To be fully received is to be nurtured, supported, and empowered as in no other way. The pinnacle of receiving and being received, however, usually comes with the experience of falling in love.

The power of receiving is the real magic of falling in love. Young lovers are natural experts at receiving. Each drinks the highest qualities of the other, each drinks the exquisite appreciation of the other. Receiving each other when falling in love, however, is a psychobiological instinct. All our conscious and hidden desires for security, sexual fulfillment, intimacy, and companionship empower us to appreciate and receive the highest in each other. The honeymoon ends at that inevitable point when some of our hidden desires are frustrated; then we may see only each other's flaws. This can seem a veritable betrayal. To once have been a god, and now to be a schmuck, is a shift in appreciation that can create plenty of hurt and resentment. Yet, paradoxically, this is the very point at which *conscious* love can begin to grow.

GROWING IN CONSCIOUS LOVE

*L*earning to receive each other *unconditionally* can breathe life into every area of a relationship. Receiving means we appreciate people for who they are, not who we would like them to be. Failing to develop this art, we will remain unconscious receivers: If my partner receives me and gives me what I want or need, I will receive my partner. If my partner closes down to me, rejects me and fails to fulfill my desires, I will react and reject my partner. Our appreciation and love for each other remains conditional.

For example, Ken came to me for counseling because he resented the fact that his wife was not interested in sex. In his efforts to rekindle their romance, he had initiated candlelit dinners, bought her flowers, and given her sexy lingerie. He had even brought home an X-rated video for them to watch together—all to little avail. He felt there must be something wrong with her, and wondered what else he could possibly do. He was surprised when I suggested not only that he do nothing more, but that he should actually suspend his expectations about sex for a couple of weeks, and simply concentrate on receiving what his wife really wanted to give. "Be open to receiving her reflections, her feelings," I suggested. "Talk with her. Give her attention. Love her for what she does offer." When Ken stopped pushing and began receiving, his wife was drawn to him once again. Ken, like many other men I have counseled, was surprised to find how this simple opening allowed his romance to revive.

Receiving also extends beyond the sphere of an intimate relationship. We can focus on receiving not only each other, but all others. Making an effort to receive others fully can be one of the most healing and transforming experiences in our lives. It is easy to judge others—their ideas, beliefs, ways of doing things. Judgment closes us down to each other, closes us down to life. By contrast, receiving can be an awakening to life. We can receive from everything—from the beauty of nature, from books, from music, from the ideas of others, from everyone we meet. As we learn to consciously receive, to drink life in, we become much more innocent, simple, and fulfilled. To receive life is to open our hearts. There is nothing more valuable on the path of love.

Receiving is such a powerful positive force in a relationship, that if even only one partner consciously opens to receiving the other, it is often enough to entirely turn a relationship around. Years ago, while teaching in the Midwest, I counseled a couple who dramatically demonstrated this.

When Sarah and Don came to me, they had been separated for over a year. They had separated with the express intention of eventually moving back together, for they both still wanted their relationship to work. Nevertheless, whenever they talked about getting back together, one particular problem arose, and they would find it impossible to reunite. They came to me because they were starting to feel they would never be able to live together.

The problem that kept them separated, by both their accounts, was that Sarah could not help herself from criticizing Don. As she put it, she could not help "hammering away at him." Granted, Don once had what most would call a lot of room for hammering. For over ten years, he had lived as a near-starving sculptor. His love was his art, and he had spent almost no attention on anything else in his life. Before Sarah and Don met, he had lost a decent job and spent several years virtually homeless, living off of friends and relatives. His car had windows that wouldn't roll down, door handles that didn't work, and thick clouds

The Art of Receiving

of exhaust spewing from the tailpipe. In a word, most of us would have handed Sarah the hammer.

Over the years, largely as a result of Sarah's constant efforts, Don had gradually taken vast strides forward in his life. He had gotten a part-time job, rented his own apartment, and learned to take care of himself and his appearance. Piece by piece, he was fixing his car. Even by Sarah's standards, his life was coming together. Yet Sarah could not stop hammering. Every time they got together, she found any number of points that needed further improving.

Sarah freely admitted that her criticism of Don was compulsive. She also knew that it was no longer working, but was only pushing Don away. After all his efforts to become more responsible, her continued criticism only injured his self-esteem. He had lost trust in her love, and he feared that she would never let him be himself. He felt that they should probably call it quits. Sarah knew all of this, but still could not help herself. In addition to criticizing Don, she constantly questioned their compatibility. She speculated that growing up with an alcoholic father who had often disappointed her had left her terrified. She could not help feeling that unless she tried to change Don, their relationship would never work—he might just be too irresponsible.

After listening to their story, I asked Sarah to relate how she felt Don had changed over the years. As she listed the ways, which literally took her six or seven minutes to recount, she softened noticeably. Then I asked her what she loved about Don. Not surprisingly, she named many of the traits that made Don so unique: his independence, his courage to be himself and to not conform, his dedication to what he believed in, his talent as an artist, his sensitivity, his softness, his love for her . . . At that point, she had to stop talking to hold back tears. After a moment, Sarah said she realized that much of what she was trying to change in Don was precisely what she loved most in him.

Once she had reconnected with her love for Don, it became clear to Sarah that if she was going to discover whether they were really compatible, she'd have to appreciate Don's uniqueness and support those qualities in him, and not constantly hammer away at him. Only then would she give Don the space to continue growing. Only then would he be able to trust in her enough to listen to her.

I discovered midway through the session that they had only allowed themselves this one hour to see if there was any hope for them. Now, with our session about to end, I asked Sarah to try to resist her tendency to judge, critique, and mold Don; to recognize that this was coming out of her fear and only destroyed her chances of ever finding out if they could have a relationship. I asked her instead to try to appreciate and love Don for his positive traits and for all the ways he was growing. Finally, I asked her to approach my suggestions as she would a spiritual discipline (Sarah had mentioned that she was involved in a particular spiritual path)—with discrimination and a firm resolve. As they were leaving, Sarah told me that she felt the session had been very humbling, but good, for her.

A week later, I got a call from Sarah. They had experienced a major breakthrough in their relationship and were looking for a house together. A month later, I saw them again, and they reported feeling like blissful newlyweds. No doubt they had many challenges ahead; still, I wish I could claim many such one-session breakthroughs.

Sarah's parting comment to me was significant: She felt humbled. At a point when their relationship looked nearly over, she surrendered, she opened to the unknown. She became receptive to the inner knowledge that it was vital for her to overcome her critical tendency—for herself as well as for their relationship.

Sarah had discovered personal meaning. She could not simply try to appreciate Don without first deeply feeling her own challenge to grow. To do so would have almost surely involved repression. First we must open ourselves to receive meaning; then we can exercise our will to enact the meaning that we genuinely feel.

When we open to the unknown, we inevitably feel humbled. Feeling humbled, we do not presume to judge others; instead, we are spontaneously more receptive to their higher qualities. The more open we are to the unknown, the more open we are to personal meaning, and the more we are freed to love.

Sometimes we may feel, "But I am justified in focusing on the negative in my partner, because it is there, it is real, and it is impossible to live with." Perhaps. But it is important to remember that we receive from each other precisely what we put our attention on. If we focus on the negative, the other person is almost certain to give us that. We thereby weaken each other, ourselves, and the relationship. Justification is not the issue, growing in love is.

No matter how intimately we have experienced the negative qualities in another person, we cannot truly know that person until we see them with the eyes of love, until we receive the highest in that person. It has been said that we cannot know someone until we know them to be who and what God knows them to be. And God, it is said, is infinite, unconditional love.

This does not, however, preclude making observations to correct and help each other. Yet this can take place within a context of appreciation. Indeed, we are only in a position to correct each other if we are also aware of each other's beauty and humanity. In that case, our correction will come from an entirely different perspective than from one of anger and blame, which negates all beauty. This is true no matter how penetrating our psychological insight may be into each other. As St. Paul puts it,

> *If I have all the eloquence of men or of angels, but speak without love, I am simply a gong booming or a cymbal clashing. If I have the gift of prophecy, understanding all the mysteries there are, and knowing everything . . . but without love, then I am nothing at all.*
>
> (1 CORINTHIANS 13:1,2)

The Art of Receiving

When we appreciate each other's uniqueness and beauty, and yet see our partner's shortcomings, we will not only correct, we will support, we will nurture.

When we judge we not only injure our partner, we injure ourselves. We become self-righteous. We lose touch with our humility as well as our love. Any sense of personal meaning instantly disappears, for it is impossible to genuinely feel personal meaning while concentrating on the faults of another.

Christ advised protection from these consequences of judging another when he suggested that we love even our enemies, and turn the other cheek. The Buddhist saint Santideva also sets an example when he admonishes himself, "Although others may do something wrong, I should transform it into a fault of my own." As extreme as this idea may seem to the secular mind, it holds a subtle wisdom. When we focus on another's fault, we are expressing our own negativity—which not only projects onto the other person, but fills our own mind. This will perpetuate a reality in which we are alienated from the experience of love.

Consider what happened to Sarah. Caught in her own fear, Sarah was unable to receive Don. As a result of her constant criticism, Don withdrew from the relationship. Thus, just as Sarah feared, Don appeared incapable of being a responsible, mature participant in the relationship. He seemed to be withdrawing from the responsibilities of the partnership, just as he had previously withdrawn from the responsibilities of his life. Her fear was truly a self-fulfilling prophecy. It projected, and helped to create, an entire reality in which love had fallen out of sight.

All this, however, was little more than a mirage (albeit a convincing one); deep down, Don and Sarah loved each other. Don had also demonstrated his commitment to moving his life ahead. If only Sarah's fear could be healed, then their love could breathe again. My work with Sarah in that session was aimed at easing and relaxing her fear so she could again receive Don. The spiritual discipline I suggested at the close of the session encouraged her to continue to concentrate on owning her fear and on healing herself. Thus she would raise her fear-based reality into one of love.

Not all the problems between Sarah and Don were Sarah's fault, of course. Though Don had come a long way in his personal life, threads of the old life still clung to him. He was not entirely understanding of Sarah's fears; by reacting to Sarah and withdrawing emotionally, he played an equal role in creating the reality of their relationship. Nevertheless, someone had to take a step. Either could have, but it seemed in this case that Sarah was the critical starting point. Had we continued counseling, Don's ongoing challenges within the relationship would certainly have come onto center stage soon enough.

When she took that step, Sarah discovered that the challenges in their relationship were perfectly calibrated to heal the fear within herself. It was as if that challenge existed for the sake of her growth. Had Don been the one to take that step, he could have experienced that the situation was entirely for his benefit.

This is a great secret of receiving as well as healing our own hearts: Every conflict or problem in a relationship holds such abundant personal meaning for each partner that either may feel the entire situation was for his or her growth alone. To heal, we need only open to this meaning. We cannot do this, however, if we project the source of our conflict onto each other. We must own our own feelings, and so move closer to the center of ourselves. There the illusions created by our hidden fears and insecurities dissolve, and we again open our hearts to the reality of our love. (It is important to add that we cannot own our feelings and receive each other simply by straining against our own reactions. Repressing negative reactions, no matter how good our intentions, closes us to our feelings, ourselves, and to each other.)

Once Sarah owned her fear, Don no longer seemed irresponsible and incapable of being in a relationship. She could receive him for who he was. Her entire experience of reality shifted—from fear to love. She discovered for herself that love is indeed the greatest healer.

As we mature on this path, we see that even the shortcomings of our partner contribute to our personal meaning. Without them, we would not have the chance to develop essential qualities, such as patience, forgiveness, tolerance, and unconditional love. We would simply have no opportunity. Just as schoolchildren need problems to sharpen their academic skills, we need to experience interpersonal problems to develop qualities of heart and character. We are each other's greatest teacher—by our shortcomings as well as by our virtues.

The more clearly we see this, the easier it becomes to look within and feel our own personal meaning. Sometimes we may resist looking within because we feel we will be taken advantage of. Ultimately, however, we look within, not for each other, but for ourselves. We become free from reaction, we find more peace within ourselves, we become free to love. It doesn't matter how our partner responds; we can cross that bridge later. First we must do for ourselves what we so readily ask each other to do: open ourselves to growth.

CREATING A UNION OF OPPOSITES

A relationship is not only a union of two unique individuals, it is a union of two unique realities, each formed by its own history of life experience. Every intimate relationship is also unique—a highly significant life experience, holding tremendous power to expand both partners. In a growing relationship, each learns and receives from the other, each grows into a more complete person who encompasses more of life. Whereas it is the nature of an intimate relationship to expand us in this way, it is also human nature to resist this expansion. All too often, we feel that our perspective alone is the right one, the best one. Instead of absorbing each other's highest qualities, we attempt to impose our own perspective on our partner. This not only short-circuits growth in a relationship, it often ends the relationship.

When we think that our version of reality is the best one, instead of appreciating and receiving the higher qualities in each other, we want our partner to manifest those same positive qualities that we possess (or think we possess). If I am conscientious in keeping a neat and clean house, I will probably want my partner to do the same. If my partner lacks my housekeeping talent, this may be a trouble spot in the relationship. If setting an example and asking nicely fail, I may well attempt to coerce my partner into living up to my standards. Such a reaction only invites resistance, resentment, and power struggles.

If, however, I open and receive my partner's strengths, then I create an atmosphere of receptivity in our relationship. Though it may still require asking more than once, my partner is much more likely to respond and eventually "absorb" my housekeeping talent. Thus we both learn from each other, and we may become more balanced and whole personalities.

In my own marriage, my wife and I have experienced such growth in many areas. One such area involved reconciling our differences in handling money. Early in our marriage, we were struggling financially. Yet, as far as I could tell, my wife seemed oblivious to this. At times it seemed to me that someone had mistaken our front porch for a loading dock for UPS. Packages were delivered regularly—clothes, toys, books, and magazines Susan had ordered for herself and the kids. She habitually kept the heat in our house to a toasty level all winter long. She was ready prey for any charitable cause that happened to call or ring our doorbell. She was quick to invite friends over for meals, even though most of our friends at that time were unmarried and never thought to return the invitation. All of these habits came naturally to Susan, but from my perspective they made it that much harder to make ends meet.

In argument after argument, I tried to impress Susan with the need for frugality. She countered that I was selfish, cheap, and controlling, and she resisted me with all her will. In fact, as far as she was concerned, hers was the cause of righteousness. Not only did she feel that I had no right to dictate to her, she was convinced that a liberal attitude toward money—trusting that all would be provided if one gave freely—was the only way to live. Likewise, I was convinced that budgeting, planning, and economizing were necessities, given our finances. We were at a total impasse. She would not budge an inch, and neither would I. Eventually, I realized that to argue the issue any further was fruitless. Our arguments were becoming so destructive that I finally gave up. I didn't like it, but I decided that I would just have to learn to live with Susan's way of handling money. For my part, I would compensate by buying nothing.

Though this was far from an ideal attitude, it did seem to help a little. With the pressure off, Susan began to display somewhat more care in her spending. We still argued about money occasionally, but for the most part, we simply accepted that we would never see eye to eye on money matters. It was not until the following Christmas, however, that we really made progress in this area.

One night, as I was getting into bed with Susan, I noticed a pile of unfamiliar department store boxes in our closet. The number and the size of the packages instantly pushed my panic button—Susan had been Christmas shopping, and I had made the ultimate blunder of neglecting to set a limit to her spending. I could not believe I had allowed this to get by me. When I asked how much she had spent on Christmas gifts, she refused to answer me. My money paranoia shot off the scale. Before you could say Ebenezer we were arguing. Finally, she told me how much she had spent, and though it was not much more than we had spent the previous year, it was twice what I would have suggested. What ensued was a major argument that threatened to ruin the holidays far more than a bloated credit card balance.

After twenty minutes of fruitless yelling back and forth, I jumped out of bed, put my boots and overcoat on over my pajamas, and took a walk in the snow to cool off. I walked for maybe half an hour. I nearly froze, but the walk did thaw out my heart. I knew this battle of the purse strings couldn't go on. Despite having vehemently argued my case, I also didn't care for the way I was feeling: stingy, uptight, and controlling. And though Susan may have spent more than I would have, in my heart I knew that her motives were not irresponsible.

For the first time in our marriage, I began to actually feel more than a glimmer of openness to Susan's perspective on money. I had come to a point of surrender—not of my integrity, but of what kept me from my integrity. I had surrendered my sense of being right, I had opened to the unknown, and there I was just beginning to rediscover my appreciation and love for Susan.

When I got back home, I apologized to Susan. I told her that I was going to watch my stinginess, and that I knew I was lucky to have someone as generous, and even as responsible with money, as she was. (After all, it could have been much worse.) That night we went to sleep minus a major roadblock to feeling our love.

An interesting truth of life comes to light when we begin to receive another person: We find that within every negative quality lies a positive quality, within every weakness lies a strength. Within what I had always perceived to be Susan's irresponsible and spendthrift attitude toward money were great strengths: her trust in life, her generosity, her social conscience, her love for family and friends, her desire to care for and give to her family. Once I opened myself to appreciate and receive these qualities in Susan, not only did my longstanding grudge against her spending begin to dissolve, but my own selfishness and anxiety about money also began to dissolve. The more I have since valued the positive qualities within Susan's approach to money, the more I have begun to feel the birth of those qualities in myself. I have not lost my ability to economize and budget, but I have become more trusting and relaxed about money. I have gained a good part of the truth that was in Susan's perspective.

Likewise, Susan has absorbed what was true in my perspective. She is still generous and trusting by nature, but she now displays all the care and responsibility in spending that I had so long hoped for. Gradually, we have both become more balanced in our attitudes toward money. We still occasionally disagree on financial issues, but since that night, almost never have those disagreements turned into heated arguments.

This type of growth has taken root in nearly every area of our lives: in our individual approaches to raising our children, housekeeping, work habits, diet, sex, recreation, and so on. Sometimes this happens gradually, naturally, almost without our even noticing. At other times it has involved conflict and effort.

We have discovered that when we are in conflict, and yet consciously make an effort to receive each other, learning from each other is so much smoother. Just applying the understanding that no one way is right, that becoming whole involves balance, can relax polarization and allow us to accept each other. By appreciating our differences, we grow, and our conflict diminishes. When we resent our differences and try to make each other conform to our own strengths, we stagnate. Then, even our strengths become weaknesses.

In many of the world's great mythologies and religions—from the book of Genesis to ancient Chinese, Greek, and Indian mythologies—we find abundant recognition that becoming whole involves a *union* of opposites within the personality. The following list illustrates some polarities we may balance in each other through an intimate relationship. The list could go on and on, for life in all its facets is characterized by pairs of opposites.

Yang	*Yin*
Intellectually oriented	Feeling oriented
Rational	Intuitive
Visual bias (visionary)	Tactile bias (sensate)
Abstract	Organic
Assertive/aggressive	Passive/receptive
Competitive	Cooperative
Emphasis on distinctions	Emphasis on harmony
Conditionally loving	Unconditionally loving
Takes care of self	Takes care of others
Questioning	Trusting
Discriminating	Accepting
Goal-oriented	Process-oriented
Perfection-oriented	Completion-oriented
Disciplinary	Nurturing
Independent	Interdependent
Spirit-oriented	Love-oriented

The dynamics of growing toward wholeness through an intimate relationship are not always straightforward, however. An intimate love relationship does not simply encourage us to embrace opposite qualities; first, it actually encourages us to polarize.

Before my marriage, I had not been overly responsible with money. If anything, I spent money carelessly and did not know the meaning of budgeting. Once married, however, Susan seemed to take over that role, adding to it a few flourishes of her own, such as her unbounded charity. I fell into the opposite role of carefully guarding the purse strings. I have seen this happen to couples time and again. If one partner becomes independent in a relationship, the other begins to feel emotionally dependent; if one withdraws from sex, the other can think about nothing else; if one assumes an intellectual, rational approach to issues in the relationship, the other swings toward an emotional/intuitive approach; if one acts as disciplinarian to the children, the other becomes protective and nurturing.

Once we define ourselves in these roles of opposition, we develop and strengthen these qualities within ourselves. This often represents an important phase in our growth as individuals. Eventually, however, we may become so identified with our own end of the spectrum that we can only see the downside of our partner's perspective. If we remain so polarized, we will eventually drift apart completely. Our growth, and the health of the relationship, then, depends upon reconciling these opposites within ourselves by reconciling ourselves to each other—by receiving each other's best qualities. In so doing, we balance our individual strengths; we become not only more accepting and loving, but wise.

Love is receptivity. Through love, man takes woman into himself and woman takes man into herself. Love balances all opposites. We become more whole by the very act of loving.

CHAPTER THREE

REAL COMMUNICATION

Creating a Communion of Feeling

*C*ommunication is love's most vital nourishment. Through communication we feel our companionship, open our hearts to each other, and deepen our intimacy.

Yet for most couples, effective communication—especially in times of stress or conflict—remains an enigma. At least part of the reason is that from the time we first learn to talk, we are conditioned to understand communication in a light virtually guaranteed to cause trouble in an intimate relationship.

We grow up with the understanding that communication means conveying our thoughts and ideas through words, and that good communication means conveying this information clearly, concisely, and persuasively. If I can communicate well in this regard, I will receive reinforcement from parents and teachers, increase my chances of success in school, and gain the respect of my peers. As an adult my communication abilities can only be an asset in my career. They may even serve me well in getting *into* a love relationship.

All that wonderful ability to communicate, however, may not help me one iota to create a fulfilling relationship—it may even become a stumbling block on the path of love. Here, as nowhere else, the observation of Lucius Seneca holds true: "The articulate voice is more distracting than mere noise."

Years ago, when I was in college, I had a professor who was an excellent communicator—in the conventional sense. A brilliant intellect, he could convey even the most abstract concepts clearly. He could argue a position so deftly that whatever side of an issue he took, it seemed the more compelling one. I later learned, however, that his great skills of communication did not serve him so well in his personal life. At his home one evening, I watched in embarrassment as he effortlessly reduced to ashes every contribution his wife made to our conversation. His tone with her was one he might take with a rather dull student. I wasn't surprised when this marriage—his third—ended in divorce the next school year.

An intimate relationship is, by definition, uniquely personal. We can communicate ideas and information all day long with friends, students, and coworkers—with anyone—but in an intimate relationship, the essence and goal of communication goes much deeper than this. Here, it is not so much an exchange of information (or even of words) that counts, but an exchange of feeling.

Real Communication

In an intimate relationship, when we communicate only information and ideas, then our communication actually violates our intention in being together. It violates our *feelings* (or our potential feelings) for each other. If we keep it up, our relationship will begin to lose its life, for its life is feeling—love. In an intimate love relationship, the purpose of communication is not just to exchange information, but ultimately to create a *communion of feeling,* to enliven and deepen the experience of loving companionship and intimacy.

This does not mean we must always talk about our feelings with watery-eyed vulnerability. We can talk about anything. Sharing our lives is one of the great joys of intimacy. Yet, in this sharing, we will always be subtly communicating feeling; indeed, every thought, word, and action communicates some feeling—good, bad, or indifferent.

It is said that the human eye is sensitive to even a single photon of light. The human heart possesses equal sensitivity. We can sense the affection within a glance, the impatience within a motion, the irritation or love within a word. We may sense the care or neglect behind an act done or left undone. How incredibly subtle and vast communication of feeling is. Everything that we do or don't do, think or don't think, say or don't say, communicates feeling. Ultimately, everything we think, say, and do communicates who we are and our capacity to feel and give love. How, then, does all this become a communion of feeling?

The answer depends on our inner experience. If we feel appreciation, attraction, or tenderness for each other, we need only express this in an appropriate way. Whether we make our feelings known through words, a touch, a hug, or a thoughtful act, we stand an excellent chance of creating a communion of feeling, for love tends to be reciprocal.

When we feel our love, and express it in some way, love becomes an active part of our lives. When we express our love, we do much more than merely communicate ideas. We awaken life in each other. We emerge from our isolation as separate individuals and feel our hearts touching. Our intimacy and companionship breathes life. If we feel our love for each other and fail to express it, we unwittingly make the statement that other things—the TV, our jobs, the children—are more important than our feelings for each other. We convey the feeling of neglect. If this neglect becomes habitual, our positive feelings for each other will atrophy.

Sometimes I become so absorbed in my responsibilities that I lose touch with my feelings for Susan. As a result, I begin to treat her without any appreciation or any feeling at all, or worse, with impatience or irritation. In such a state, everything I say, do, or think—even just my being—is deadening to our relationship. She picks up on my feelings. She can't help it. Thankfully, she is understanding enough to give me a large margin for error when I'm feeling that way. Yet, if I neglect our relationship for too long, I definitely pay the price. We both do.

Real Communication

Even in such circumstances, we are not powerless to enliven our intimacy. It simply means we must become more self-aware, and recognize that what we are feeling or not feeling is communicating something corrosive to our relationship and to our happiness together. This simple awareness will open our heart, and we will feel naturally drawn to express our love in some way—with a hug, a loving word, a few minutes spent together. This small but potent communion can entirely refresh the chemistry of feeling between us.

At other times, I feel numb in my heart altogether. I simply feel nothing. Over the years, however, I have found that if I make some effort to consciously receive Susan—to see just one positive quality, appreciate some aspect of her caring for myself or the children, try to notice her humanness, or simply remind myself of how much we have shared together over the years—I will usually ignite a spark of love for her. Communicating this appreciation has often begun a chain reaction of love between us.

Sometimes, however, we are not preoccupied, not numb, but actively feeling hurt, angry, or resentful. We don't *want* to receive each other. Ironically, it is often at these times that we feel most compelled to communicate. We can't *wait* to express our feelings. So what if asking our partner to commune with our anger is like asking them to hug a cactus!

But what are we to do? We cannot simply shut down, repressing our feelings. Stewing is also corrosive to our relationship. When we close down to each other, we are still communicating—we are saying that we do not care enough about the relationship to work things through. Not communicating when we feel deeply hurt or reactive is perhaps the deadliest detour we can take on the path of intimacy.

This, then, is the greatest challenge of communication: creating communion when it is seemingly beyond our power to feel anything positive, when all we feel is reaction. Then communication must itself become a path to healing.

COMMUNICATION CAN HEAL

*J*n *The Art of Loving,* Eric Fromm writes, "Love is possible only if two persons communicate with each other from the center of their existence, hence if each one of them experiences himself from the center of his existence." In this line we have the key to transforming communication into both healing and communion.

Communication can heal. We don't have to always be feeling our love in order to experience a rich intimacy and companionship. We can be angry, hurt, jealous, resentful. It doesn't matter. No matter what we are feeling, we can heal and experience a communion of feeling if we are willing to do just one thing: first commune with our *own* feelings.

I may be aware of only my anger, but my anger is never the bottom line. Underneath this I may also feel any number of other feelings: hurt, fear, insecurity, jealousy. Somewhere underneath my anger, perhaps lying dormant, is also my love. For communication to become a communion of feeling, I need only open to all the layers of my feelings. I need only find the underlying core of my feelings. This core of feeling is where I am vulnerable and more fully human. Communicating from the core of our feelings invites communion, because it is here that we are most attractive.

Communicating in this way is a path in itself to becoming more human and whole. Even preparing to communicate becomes a path of healing. When we take the time to honestly feel all that we are feeling, we find our center, we find ourselves. Once we find the core of our feelings, we may discover that what we were so upset about has melted into oblivion. I can remember many times when I was furious with Susan, but took a few minutes to settle down and connect with myself before blasting her. Surprisingly, nearly every time my anger dissipated, I found myself wanting to apologize to her for something *I* had said or done.

In the next chapter, we will discuss in detail how we can not only connect with the core of our feelings, but heal ourselves emotionally by virtue of our own awareness. As a preparation to communicate on an issue of tension, this process is invaluable. Nevertheless, sometimes we do not have time to prepare to communicate. Still, if we are willing to commune with our own feelings, even as we speak to each other, we can heal ourselves and our relationship. When we open not only to our immediate reactions, but to all that underlies those reactions, the entire nature of our communication changes.

THE MIRACLE OF VULNERABILITY

*C*ommunication as communion is truly a function of vulnerability. This means opening to the full range of our feelings. The deeper the vulnerability, the more profound the communion.

About ten years ago, while I was offering a relationship workshop in the Minneapolis area, a woman asked me if I would privately tutor her and her husband in communication skills. Their problems had brought them to the brink of divorce. Tina was an intelligent woman in her early thirties, and had recently reentered school to receive training as a legal secretary. Mike, a construction worker, was quiet, reserved, and extremely bright. They had four children. At our first session, I asked each what they wanted to get out of working with me and what they saw as the main challenge in their relationship. Tina said her desire was for a real relationship. For years, she felt that they hadn't had one. She said that Mike never communicated, never opened up to her. He was like a brick wall, and she could never get through. She admitted that in her frustration, she was in an almost constant state of anger. The least little thing would set her off. She would start in on him for something, and he would not respond; she would start screaming, and he would shake his head, walk into the next room, and close the door. She volunteered that the only reason she hadn't left Mike was for the sake of the children, and because she needed his income to finance her schooling.

At this verbal slap in the face, I expected Mike to jump out of his chair, but he seemed completely unmoved—smiling, arms crossed on his chest. He calmly waited for me to ask him what he would like to achieve in our sessions.

He responded that he just wanted to be able to live in the same house with Tina, that he did not have any expectation for a love relationship, but only wanted a businesslike coexistence with her for the sake of parenting their children. In response to Tina's characterization of him as a brick wall, he said that whenever he had tried to open up in the past, she would fly into a rage. He had learned that he could not tell her what he really felt. He added that even when he had agreed to marry her many years ago, he had not been able to communicate his real feelings because of her rage. Then he returned Tina's verbal slap: He claimed that he had actually never loved her, and had only married her because she had pushed, pulled, and tugged him into it—and because she had been pregnant.

Here was a great example of crystal clear communication creating anything but a communion of feeling.

Since Mike claimed to have no interest in a love relationship, Tina agreed that they should just learn some communication skills so they could be civil to each other for the sake of their children. For the remainder of that session and the next, we attempted to do just that, with predictably dubious results. In the third session, however, something unexpected happened.

When they arrived that day, Tina seemed particularly disturbed. Mike was calm, as usual. They had been fighting (or rather, Tina had been fighting, and Mike had been closing down) all week long about how much candy, sodas, and other sweets Mike allowed their kids to consume. Tina was adamant that the kids only have desserts after a meal, and healthy (non-sweet) snacks between meals. The task of controlling this in the evenings, however, fell to Mike, since Tina was in school. Mike maintained that Tina's expectations were unrealistic and far too strict. This issue had flared up regularly in recent months, and had never been resolved. We decided to use this for our exercise in communication.

They spent the first few minutes arguing back and forth, justifying their own positions, and ignoring most of what we had discussed about effective communication. Like most marital spats, the overall tone was heated, blaming, and defensive. I sat by and watched for a while, since at least Mike was talking. Finally, I interrupted and asked Mike how he felt about the situation. At first he began iterating his position, but again I interrupted him. I asked him how he *felt*. He knew what I meant from our previous sessions. The idea behind this communication exercise was to allow one person the chance to uninterruptedly communicate all the layers of their feelings about the situation—not just their immediate reactions—including any deeper feeling of which they became aware. I asked him to tell Tina, not me, what he felt about the situation.

He was quiet for a few moments, then began, "I have tried to control the kids and how much candy they eat," he said, looking at Tina, "but they just eat it anyway, or sneak it when I'm not watching. They don't listen to me like they do to you. I don't know why. Maybe you're just more strict than I am."

He took a deep breath. "I guess I feel hurt that you blame me for something that is not all my fault," he said, his face turning red. "I know I could do more about it," he continued, still looking at Tina, "but I can't help feeling resistant to you when you tell me what to do."

Tina and I waited to see if he would say anything more. Nearly a minute passed.

"I have wondered why the kids don't listen to me," he continued in a soft voice, "I guess I do feel some insecurity about it; I've wondered if maybe I'm not a good father in some ways." His voice quavered slightly.

"How would you like it to be, Mike?" I asked quietly after a moment.

For perhaps half a minute, he was silent. His face looked softer than I'd ever seen him. "I'd like us to have a normal family," he said finally, looking down. "Yeah, a normal family, with some real love."

He glanced up at Tina. She was already looking at him with amazement and a hint of softness in her face.

"I do care about you," he told her quietly.

"I know," she whispered.

I had witnessed a minor miracle of vulnerability. Mike and Tina had given their love up for dead (so had I), and suddenly signs of life were stirring. Within a couple more minutes of conversation, they had agreed on guidelines for when the kids could have candy and how much. Agreement came effortlessly, gracefully.

I wish I could say that all of their problems were solved in that session, but it's not true. By the time they came back the following week, they were back in the same old patterns (though the candy issue was working out). Nevertheless, even if only for a few minutes, the resentments and illusions that had held their relationship for years disappeared. The more vulnerable Mike became at each stage of communication, the more he drew Tina toward him. They had gotten beneath all the built-up hardness and had tasted the reality of love.

Over the years, I have seen countless conflicts turn into communion. I have seen couples grow in unexpected ways—*once they opened to the depths of their own feelings.* Conflict over an issue is never simply an unfortunate obstacle to our happiness. It is a powerful opportunity to grow and heal. Conflict can become a gift to a relationship, a gift to each partner. This conflict over candy became a chance for Mike to connect with and express all of the layers of his feelings, for the first time in their relationship. As small as it may seem, for Mike this was a momentous step in the direction of learning to love. We can only love each other once we open to the depths of our own heart.

In the beginning of the session, before I interrupted Mike and Tina, they were simply arguing, blaming, reacting with anger and defensiveness. They were totally at odds. They had their shields up and were in the midst of combat. In the fury of battle, they took little heed of the wounds they were inflicting or receiving. The level of vulnerability was virtually nil (except, of course, that at least they were talking).

Most of us also vent immediate reactions of anger and think we are communicating. We are not communicating. We are failing to communicate with each other because we are failing to communicate with ourselves. Consider what Mike eventually admitted to feeling: pain, insecurity, responsibility, caring. Somewhere inside his anger and defensiveness were all of these other feelings, lying silently in the background. Tina and Mike could not really listen to each other's reactions, but Tina could hear Mike's deeper feelings with ease.

Unfortunately, when we are angry and defensive, we can't afford to connect with such deeper feelings. We need to make our point, be right, protect ourselves. Communicating only our anger and blame shows we have lost touch with our ultimate purpose in communicating. Instead of moving toward a communion of feeling, we want to be right, or worse, we want to blast each other. That is our apparent intention, and this is just what we do. Usually, the result is an angry and defensive response, polarized positions, and bad feelings. This is the power of intention. By our intention, we create our lives and our relationship.

To make communication a communion of feeling, we need to interrupt the intention to be right or to blast each other, and consciously reconnect with our ultimate intention in being together: to enjoy the benefits of a rich, intimate companionship. Reconnecting with this intention alters the destiny of our communication. It does not mean repressing our anger, but finding what is within our anger. It means bringing our conflict onto the path of love by going beneath our immediate reactions, and opening to all that we are feeling.

Once Mike put his sword and shield down and began exploring his feelings, he noticed almost immediately that he was hurting. Once we stop arguing and look within, we are likely to find pain. We become aware of the wounds that have been inflicted. Whatever made us angry in the first place may have hurt us, and often our arguing has hurt us. Letting ourselves feel this pain and then express it is the beginning of the vulnerability that will turn conflict into potential communion.

I imagine that Tina was relieved to hear Mike say that he felt hurt. This was so much more open and human than acting like a brick wall, or arguing his position. Being told how you have unwittingly hurt the person closest to you is a welcome relief after being emotionally shut out of your partner's life for years. Hearing how you have unwittingly hurt the person closest to you is also much easier to listen to than an angry attack. Still, Mike was communicating some sense of blame: *Tina* had hurt him. A deep communion of feeling is not guaranteed if we stay at this level of vulnerability. We need to go even deeper.

Mike's admission that he probably could do more to control the children's sugar intake was another step in the right direction. Just a few moments before, he would never have admitted this. This statement bordered on accepting some responsibility for the situation. It showed a degree of openness. Yet again, he maintained that Tina's demanding attitude was interfering with his parenting. He was not yet fully accepting his responsibility.

Notice that we could have stopped at this point and used Mike's admission to try to work toward a compromise. I could have interrupted him and asked, "All right, Mike, so if Tina eases up on her demands, would you feel better about limiting how much candy the kids eat?" Yet this would have deprived Mike of the chance to fully open to his feelings. We might have resolved the immediate conflict. Yet the sense of personal meaning Mike gained in acknowledging his insecurity as a parent would never have occurred. Neither would he have felt and expressed his desire for a loving relationship and his caring for Tina.

In an intimate relationship, compromise is not always the best solution. Compromise can be useful in working out the details of a situation. Yet, if we do not feel our love in compromising, we have compromised ourselves. We have taken care of details, but neglected our relationship.

When we fail to use a conflict for our growth and healing, we stray from the path of personal meaning. Instead of feeling a deepened intimacy, we invisibly sap our relationship of life. As Tina and Mike found after the exercise, compromise comes effortlessly, gracefully, once we are connected with our core feelings.

Mike's next step in this direction came as he admitted to feeling insecure as a father. These few words, however brief, totally changed the course of the communication. Mike dropped all blame of Tina and honestly explored his own feelings. Revealing these feelings required a quantum leap in vulnerability. He truly had put down his sword and shield and had bared his soul. As of that moment, Tina and Mike were no longer combatants, but potential companions. By exploring his responsibility with such vulnerability, Mike was also drawing Tina into more openness, into her heart.

To some, this may seem beyond the call of duty on Mike's part. Normally in a conflict, we just want to settle things. As a result of our intention only to resolve the situation, however, we become obsessed with thoughts of who was right and who was wrong, of fairness, of our personal rights. We hold each other accountable. We do not think of growth. We do not think of our ultimate purpose in communicating as a couple—a communion of feeling. Instead,

we get caught in cycles of reacting to each other and fighting for what we want or what we think we deserve.

Looking within, as Mike did here, breaks these cycles.
By acknowledging his insecurity as a parent, Mike began to
discover personal meaning within the situation. Here was
a direction for him as a father: to apply himself to become a
more responsible parent. His insecurity, as long as it went
unacknowledged, contributed to his poor self-image and
made him feel incapable of communicating with Tina. This
was at the root of his reactions to Tina. Having found his
insecurity, having opened to it, having looked at it and accepted its meaning, he began to be freed from it. He became stronger, more open, more sensitive, just by facing it.
By so doing, he also brought the communication between
them to an entirely new level.

One of the great landmarks of vulnerability in communication is the point at which we can admit to our own
responsibility. Initially, we may think we have very little responsibility, only to realize later that ours was the greater
share. No matter how small we may think our responsibility is at first, we should make an effort to find it. Sometimes it may seem frightening to become so vulnerable. It
may seem too dangerous: What if I am crushed by my partner's insensitivity? What if my partner takes no responsibility? Vulnerability does entail risk. Yet, if we have any
hope of a growing relationship, we must take that risk.
(Nonetheless, if you try this a few times and don't get an
appropriate response, I recommend seeking counseling as

a couple. If your partner won't agree to counseling, go alone. You should never persist in the hope of intimacy if you are feeling emotionally battered.)

This raises an important question. Mike was doing all the work. What about Tina? Mike may have acted like a brick wall, but she flew into rages. Further, maybe she was being unreasonably strict with the kids' diet. First, this was a ground rule in this particular communication process: Each person gets to speak without interruption. This gives the person speaking the chance to explore their feelings, with the result that one person does "do all the work" of looking within first. Nevertheless, even at home, we need to each be willing to take the first step of looking within.

I have often been told I am lucky to have Susan as a wife, and I am. She will look within and find her responsibility in a situation, even when her share is only a fraction of mine. I am lucky to have someone so committed to growth. We should all make each other so lucky. Far from putting us at a disadvantage, looking within and accepting our responsibility in a situation, no matter how slight, not only opens us to growth, but powerfully invites the other person to find their responsibility. It is human nature. If one person apologizes, chances are that the other person will also apologize. It doesn't matter how stubbornly entrenched both parties were one minute before, vulnerability invites vulnerability.

After all, if we make an effort to look within only when we know we are in the wrong, how often will we look within? How often are we ready and willing to admit that our partner is right and we are wrong? Most of us feel we are in the right most of the time–at least when it comes to conflicts in an intimate relationship. If we wait to open to our opportunities for growth and healing until we are certain that our partner is right and we are wrong, then we will not do much growing. With this attitude we make our growth dependent on our partner's near perfection. But we are dependent upon each other's *imperfections* if we are to ever rise above conditional love. Our willingness to look within, regardless of each other's shortcomings, is essential to gain the freedom to love unconditionally.

The final stage of Tina and Mike's communication came when Mike expressed his caring for Tina, and Tina in return revealed her caring for him. Though Mike had done all the talking, just observing and feeling Mike's vulnerability had opened Tina's heart to Mike. Communication moving toward communion creates a powerful chemistry of feeling that literally draws both partners into their hearts. This is the power and beauty of vulnerability.

Yet vulnerability alone is not enough. We also need to express our feelings in some way. Mike could have just looked at Tina at the end without saying anything, but then she could have only guessed what he felt. By telling her that he cared about her, she knew what he felt. She had not heard these words in years. Hearing them helped open her heart to Mike.

When we begin to feel even the first stirrings of affection, we should express it in some way. We should not hold back or play it safe. For most of us, love is the easiest feeling to commune with. Our love is precisely what we want to experience, so we should express it, either verbally—"I love you," "I just want us to support each other, to feel our love"—or nonverbally, by touching, holding hands, hugging. This is a final step of vulnerability into communion.

Once they were feeling from their center, Mike readily agreed to Tina's guidelines for how much candy was appropriate for the kids. Communication as a communion does not mean that we cannot also work out the practical details of a situation. Again, once we feel our love for each other, agreement will usually come quite effortlessly, without the need for tough negotiating and bargaining. Polarization dissolves. We may even end up sympathizing with each other's point of view more than our own. When communication creates communion, we not only experience our love, we open to each other's perspectives. We receive each other, become more balanced and whole.

This phenomenon raises a fascinating aspect of communication: Reality itself changes, depending on what we are feeling.

When we are angry, we feel that the other person is at fault. We feel compelled to correct, criticize, and blame. Our partner may seem to have no redeeming qualities at all. We may be convinced that we have never loved each other. We may want to end the relationship.

Then, as we connect with our pain, we may feel how unfortunate the situation is; we cannot believe it is happening to us; we wish it were not happening. We may wish we could change it, but we feel powerless to do so.

Once we connect with our underlying fears and insecurities, we begin to understand each other's perspective. Suddenly, our partner doesn't look so terrible. We see our own responsibility; we see our own challenge to grow; we may even express remorse for how we have acted.

Finally, in an experience of love, we sense each other's humanness; we feel appreciation for the same person whom a moment before we couldn't stand. We realize that all we really want is to feel united. We may even feel thankful for the conflict, which allowed us to see something about ourselves and draw us closer in a fresher experience of tenderness and intimacy. The entire conflict may even seem a gift of grace.

Earlier we discussed how we can only know each other through love. When we are caught in negative reactions, we are in a distorted reality. We do not know the truth of ourselves or of the situation. How much more difficult it is, therefore, to work out practical details. Thus not only do we experience reality differently, but we *create* different realities at different levels of feeling. Tina and Mike had created the reality of their relationship based on their feelings of antagonism. With their love, they felt the glimmering of a new, potential reality.

Reality is different at different levels of feeling; only through the vulnerability that allows communication to become communion can we discover for ourselves what is Real.

THE HEALING POWER OF LISTENING

*L*istening is essential if communication is to become communion. Only our willingness to listen
to each other offers the safety to open to and express the
core of our feelings. Had Tina interrupted Mike before he
had finished exploring his feelings in our session, they
might still be arguing about their kids' diet.

Several years ago my wife and I experienced a healing
and breakthrough in our relationship more powerful than
anything we had ever experienced together. It started with
the simple act of listening. We had just returned from a
three-week vacation together, during which we had found
a deep renewal of our love. A day or two later, however,
Susan became inexplicably irritable over little things. At
one point she seemed to me irrationally angry because I
had not yet washed and vacuumed the car after our vacation. Normally, I reacted to her irritability with irritability
of my own. This time, however, I responded from a deeper
level. I saw that she was not happy, that she needed help.
Instead of reacting, I felt compassion for her.

I asked her if she wanted to sit down and talk. Sensing
that I was outside my normal pattern of reaction, she immediately softened. I put my arm around her, and gently
asked what she was feeling. She was quiet for a few moments. Finally, she simply said, "I don't know." Then she
began to cry. I held her. Within a few minutes she became

like a small girl in my arms, and somehow the meaning of her pain came to me without her telling me. It related to her sorrow over her mother's death when Susan was ten years old.

This was not an issue that regularly came up in our relationship. In fact, the subject of her mother's death had only come up once in a great while. For whatever reason, though, it seemed to be coming up now. Within a few moments, Susan told me that she was remembering how she felt when her mother had died. "Why did you go, why did you leave me, I wish I could feel your arms around me," she said between sobs. I felt her inconsolable sorrow, the sorrow of a child of ten who had lost her mother. It was the agonizing, unanswerable question, "Why?" that had left such a deep wound in her being, a wound that had never healed.

As I held her, we cried together, for I also felt inexpressible pain over the unanswerable question, "Why?" We were together like that for over an hour. Wave after wave of sorrow welled up, and then receded. After each wave there was peace. Then the sorrow would come again, and I was her father, holding the young girl who had been so wounded by the loss of her mother. I was not only her father and husband, but I felt her sorrow with her. Then again the peace would come.

Each time the wave of sorrow receded, the peace we shared seemed deeper and sweeter. Finally, the sorrow receded one last time, and the peace that followed was as indescribable and inexplicable as the agonizing question, "Why?" had seemed just a short while before. Susan later said that the phrase "the peace that passeth all understanding" had come to her during that last wave of peace.

This experience left us closer than ever. In its wake we felt our supreme caring for and union with each other. This bond was all the deeper from the knowledge that we had experienced a tremendous healing together. Susan later expressed that she felt that it was not just me who had held her, but God, and He had taken a hardness out of her heart.

There is no doubt that love is the greatest therapy. We may sometimes be called on to show our love through our willingness to listen, even in the face of our partner's seeming negativity. The effect of such listening, as in this case, can be profoundly healing.

To have someone listen to us when we are reacting is rare. We are much more used to not being heard when we are expressing anger or resentment. We are used to having our partner's defenses spring up before we can even complete our thought. By reacting to each other, we in effect reject each other and what we are feeling. We force each other to bottle up our emotions, which only makes them more explosive. If we refuse to listen, if we reject our partner when they unload, then just as healing as the process of communication might have been, that is how destructive it can become.

It is interesting that this incident occurred after our vacation, just when we were feeling much more love than usual. Why would Susan pick this time to make a display of anger?

The very moment a person feels safe and loved may be just the opportunity for repressed emotion to arise. Feeling loved, the person subconsciously senses a chance to be unburdened of repressed emotion. The display of anger is like testing the water. "Am I really loved? Can I really let this out?" If their partner reacts at this point, the person closes down—back to status quo. If, however, the partner can listen with compassion, if they can see this emotion coming up as an opportunity for their partner's healing, then it *becomes* an opportunity for healing.

This is a great secret: Once in an intimate relationship, we no longer feel entirely independently of each other. We feel in a chemistry of shared feeling, and we experience ourselves and each other in that chemistry of shared feeling. As love or compassion is introduced into that chemistry, the potential for emotional healing is awakened. The love of the listener actually creates a healing chemistry.

This is another reason why communication is so important in an intimate relationship. Susan might not have said anything to me about my failure to clean the car. She might have just fussed and fumed to herself. In that case, she never would have become aware of her hidden pain begging to be healed. Communication opens the door to healing.

Yet it is not just any listening that allows for healing. Had I taken her complaint at face value and like a good (but obtuse) husband said, "No problem, I'll clean the car," we both would have missed out. I had to notice that she was feeling pain underneath her irritation. For healing to take place, we have to attend to each other's feelings.

Still, *how* we attend to each other's feelings also counts. More likely than not, had I played the armchair psychologist, trying to cure or analyze her, I would have bombed. I would have come off too detached, too invulnerable or "in my head" to invite her subconscious pain to the surface. Rather, it is the genuine caring of the listener, the depth of their compassion, which invites the trust and vulnerability that allows emotional healing to take place.

I don't mean to encourage anyone to express negativity toward their partner in the hope of transformational healing. To be listened to when we are caught in a reaction is a gift of love. We cannot take it for granted. We should do our best to use it wisely, and find our way to the core of our feelings. It is only at the point that we become vulnerable to our deeper, underlying feelings that we can heal.

Imagine if everyone in the world understood this and listened with love. Conflict, prejudice, and war would become obsolete, for it is when we refuse to hear each other that we create the pressures of reactive negativity that explode into conflict.

Nevertheless, it is not easy for most of us to listen while our partner unloads. We may be able to stand and quietly hear our partner's grievances. We may be able to keep our mouths closed in a tight smile while we are boiling inside, but this will not create a healing chemistry. We need to listen with a healing intention, with true compassion. As difficult as this may seem, as we heal ourselves, as we see each other healing, it gradually becomes a real possibility.

Our ability to aid in each other's healing is the mark of our deepening. We are able to see through surface reactions and respond with understanding and compassion, for we see the deeper sources of pain in each other. We thus rise above reaction and judgment. Nevertheless, if this becomes merely an ideal for which we strive with great effort against our own anger and defensiveness, then we will neither allow the other person to heal through our listening, nor will we allow ourselves to heal. We cannot force this growth of compassion in ourselves. An innocent intention to develop our love is enough.

Listening with love can start in little ways. We all have days when we feel irritable. If our partner is having one of those days, we may not feel compassion, but at least we do not need to take their irritability personally. We can simply recognize that they are having an off day. This is the beginning of discrimination. We are creating a context within our relationship wherein we allow each other a margin for error. Gradually, we will find ourselves seeing not the negativity within the person, but the person behind the negativity, whom we still love. This is only one step away from spontaneously and compassionately intending to aid in that person's healing.

Seeing the truth that we are both in a process of growth and healing together is just that: a seeing, a spontaneous perception or discrimination. It cannot be merely an intellectual idea, but must arise from a direct discrimination on the level of our hearts. Love awakens the possibilities for healing, and this cannot be contrived. Our hearts are too sensitive to each other to be fooled. With a sensitivity as great as the human eye, our heart will know if the chemistry is ripe for healing. Our responsibility, then, if we wish to help each other heal, is to heal ourselves.

COMMUNICATING NATURALLY

"Techniques" of communication, as the word suggests, often feel unnatural and tend to require great discipline to put to use. I prefer that couples see the pattern of natural, healthy communication as it leads to communion and try to be aware of that pattern before and during communication over an issue of tension. This awareness is often enough to keep communication moving toward communion in a natural way. Try to remember some of the following points the next time you and your partner find yourselves in conflict.

➤ Try not to blast each other with immediate reactions. If you can, do not even open up the issue until you spend some time by yourself preparing to communicate (we'll talk about this in detail in the next chapter). Don't use this time to refine your arguments, but to find the core of your feelings. Write in a journal if you find that helpful.

➤ Once you have connected with your deeper feelings, see if you can find your responsibility in the situation, however minute it may at first seem.

➤ If you still feel it's important to talk about the situation, let your partner know that you want to talk, and make a date to talk within a reasonable time period.

➤ Describe the situation as you experienced it. Express your feelings. If you want to mention your anger do so, but don't dwell on it. Speak from the clarity and integrity you have found in connecting with the core of your feelings. Try not to slip back into surface reactions.

➤ Let your partner know any deeper, hidden feelings you experienced relating to the situation, such as insecurity, fear, guilt, or anxiety. Let your partner know of any responsibility you feel you have for the situation.

➤ If your partner reacts to anything you say, try to recognize that the reaction comes from deeper, hidden feelings. As much as possible, listen with patience and understanding, without interrupting.

➤ At whatever point you begin to actually feel your love for your partner, express it in some way.

➤ If appropriate, once you feel your love (preferably not before), discuss any practical details and clarify responsibilities so that conflicts over the same issue do not reoccur. Be careful not to grab at solutions you formulated when angry; be willing to discover fresh solutions within your present experience of love.

CHAPTER FOUR

HEALING THE HEART

Creating a New Reality

I recently saw two psychologists on TV discussing their research on marriage. They had identified two prominent danger signals by which they claimed they could predict with impressive accuracy whether or not a relationship was going to last. The first sign of danger was a pattern of escalating arguments. The second was a pattern of avoidance of all conflict, an unwillingness to deal with problems as they arose.

I was struck by the fact that both of these danger signals are symptoms of the same problem: an unwillingness to feel the full range of one's own feelings. When we will not connect with our feelings, we either lash out in reaction or we repress emotion; we either have heated arguments or we close down. Either way, we only allow ourselves to experience a small portion of our emotional being. If we cannot share our emotions with ourselves, we cannot share ourselves with others. We have no chance for communion.

Sharing our full emotional depth, however, does not mean simply letting everything hang out the moment we feel it. If I vent anger at my wife, I am not sharing my full emotional depth; I am only sharing my immediate, surface reaction. In order to share my full emotional depth, I must first experience it *myself.*

I will never forget the first time I consciously connected with the center of my feelings. Some years ago, I was working in my office at home when I overheard Susan telling our daughter to do her chores. From the tone of Susan's voice, and from the subsequent sounds of pans clanging, cupboards slamming, and occasional moans and groans of despair, I gathered she was feeling somewhat harried. Then came my turn. Popping her head in my office, she hit me with a verbal one-two punch: "What are your papers doing in the living room?" she asked in a cutting tone. Before I could answer, she added, "I could really use some help cleaning up before dinner." Then she closed my door and was gone.

I immediately felt irritated—not with her requests, but with her tone, which I didn't feel I deserved. I had reacted to Susan in this way many times in the past; and inevitably, whenever I would confront her about her tone of voice, we would end up arguing. This time, however, I caught myself. I could see that she was having a bad day, and harping on her would only make it worse. Still, I could not shake my reaction of irritation. I closed my eyes, intent on letting my anger just dissipate.

Healing the Heart

It didn't just dissipate, however. Within a few moments, my irritation gave way to an uneasy, nameless sense of fear or anxiety that I had not expected. I felt almost curious about where this anxiety was coming from, so I continued to sit, allowing myself to feel the puzzling fear. Within a few more moments, the fear took a form: I was afraid that Susan was going to try to change me. This thought was not the product of any self-analysis, it was not even an intuition; it just came to me, as if on its own.

I followed my instincts and continued to sit with this fear, knowing that I was discovering something valuable. Within another few moments, my feelings again transformed. My fear gave way to a sense of anguish: a painful feeling of insecurity that seemed to suggest that indeed something did need fixing in me—that I was not good enough. With this sense of anguish I felt a physical sensation of pressure and constriction in my chest.

This feeling of insecurity was familiar, though I had never before experienced it so intensely. In the past, whenever my sense of insecurity had come up, I would push it away, reassuring myself of my self-worth. If this insecurity was stirred by criticism coming from another person, I would counter with a few cutting observations of my own. Now I *saw* that this anxiety and insecurity were at the root of a whole set of emotional responses that kept me constricted, defensive, and closed off. I sensed that if I could fully be with this sense of anguish, even embrace what I was feeling, that I would get to the bottom of it and be released from it. Again I followed my instincts.

For maybe ten minutes, the sense of anguish came and went in waves. Sometimes the experience was intense; then it would fade. At moments I felt on the verge of tears, but they never quite came. Gradually, the anguish faded and dissolved. I felt a distinct loosening and relaxing in my chest.

What I felt next was as unexpected as everything I had experienced to that point: An indescribable sense of bliss and peace flooded through me. My whole emotional being felt renewed, innocent, free, opened. I knew that something had been healed that had been restricting me for much of my life, and I felt reconnected with the depths of myself. I felt a warm sense of being cared for, as if I was truly loved by God.

For a few more minutes, I sat and savored what I was feeling. Finally, I opened my eyes and became aware of the sounds of Susan preparing dinner in the kitchen. I felt a wave of love for her. My irritation had been entirely replaced with compassion for her and how she was feeling.

I went downstairs and found Susan busy at the stove, her back turned toward me. I walked up behind her, gently held her shoulders, turned her toward me, and gave her a hug. For a moment she remained tight, then she melted into me. We hugged silently for perhaps half a minute. I told her I loved her. Then I cleaned up my papers and helped her with the dinner. For the rest of the evening, we were both softer, more centered, more ourselves.

This was a rather dramatic example of the fruits of communing with our own feelings. Yet since then, both my wife and I, as well as many of my clients and couples who have attended my workshops, have had countless similar experiences of emotional healing. Many couples feel the lack of a true sense of intimacy in their relationship. Here is the solution: become intimate with ourselves. When we do this fully, completely, we find ourselves opening more fully to each other.

HOW WE CREATE OUR OWN REALITY

*T*he above experience was my first vivid recognition of how we create the reality of our relationships—of how we create the reality of our lives. Consider what would have happened had I simply jumped into communicating from the level of my initial irritation. What if I had chased Susan and confronted her for her negative tone? What if I had snapped back that I was already going to pick up my papers and didn't need a reminder? Things would have turned out quite differently. I can say that for certain, because in the early years of our marriage, I tried that dozens of times. Inevitably, we ended up arguing.

Further, by acting out of my irritation, I would not only have reinforced Susan's negative perception of me, but reinforced my deeper fears and insecurity at the source of my reaction. Had I reacted, suddenly Susan would not simply be having a rough day and need my love and support.

Her irritation would have found a convenient focus: me and how I was acting—defensive, unloving, unsupportive. Her negative perception of me as a self-absorbed, uncaring husband would have been confirmed. Likewise, the feedback I would have gotten would then have been precisely the content of my hidden fear: that I wasn't good enough, that I needed fixing.

Again, when we act while dislocated from the core of ourselves, we perpetuate the very same insecurities we are subconsciously avoiding. Those around us will respond to our actions in ways that also perpetuate our hidden insecurities. Susan undoubtedly felt the need to pop her head in my room in the first place because of the history of our relationship: How loving or unloving, supportive or unsupportive, I had been throughout our relationship all contributed to her perception of me as requiring a good shove. She was subconsciously responding to a thousand subtle cues, the sum of which added up to the perceived need that unless she complained to me, I probably wouldn't take the initiative to give her the support she needed. In turn, my ability to give her that support was limited by my ailing self-esteem. Why didn't I voluntarily help her, or at least comfort her, when I first heard that she was having a bad day? I was not strong enough in myself to give in this way. It was much easier to avoid her. Thus we were both unwittingly caught in a cycle of action and reaction. We had created the emotional climate—the reality—in which we were living together.

Whatever grace it was that spurred me to close my eyes and discover and heal my underlying feelings also allowed me to begin to *recreate* that reality. When I emerged from my experience of inner healing, I was able to spontaneously act in a way that was healing for both of us. I did something that was uncharacteristically nonreactive and loving, something that expressed a higher level of self-esteem. Expressing my love and supporting Susan not only helped her, but reinforced self-esteem for both of us. I experienced that I could give love; Susan experienced that she was worthy of receiving love. When one partner takes a step by acting from their core, it is healing for both partners. By finding the core of our feelings, a relationship becomes a path of inner healing.

This experience taught me that the challenges we experience in our relationships, and in our lives, are the projections of our own emotional and mental being. We may see others as the source of our misery, but we create our own reality—for better when we are authentically located in the core of our feelings, and for worse when we are not.

Parents often see this clearly in their children. We now have two daughters. Our oldest daughter went through a difficult period for much of grade school, during which she had great difficulty making friends. She was shy, withdrawn, and in a social situation she would hardly speak to any of the other children. We shared a great deal of grief with her during that period of her life, watching, supporting, and coaching until finally she outgrew that stage. Our other daughter, however, has always been on the opposite end of the scale. From the time she could walk, she made friends wherever she went. If we were in a restaurant, she would disappear and we would find her engaging another family in conversation. When she sees someone walking by our house, she often runs out and begins talking with them. Other children flock to her at school (and when they don't, she doesn't care). As parents, it is so clear that our daughters each create her own reality. Yet when it comes to ourselves, we find it much harder to see.

This raises a key question: If we know that we create our own reality, why is it so difficult to change our behavior? The answer has to do with how we form our sense of self, and reveals the depth of the feelings we need to heal.

How We Form a Sense of Self

Although genetic factors are clearly a part of our basic sense of self, psychologists inevitably point to the earliest experiences of infancy as primary in the formation of the personality. As infants we first discover ourselves in relation to our world. As infants we first discover the boundaries of our physical being, and begin to formulate the boundaries of our own identity.

As infants, in relationship with our parents, we gain our first impressions of the world as friendly and nurturing, as impersonal and unresponsive, or as a combination of these—as inconsistent. Early on, then, we discover not only how loving and nurturing the world is, but also how worthy we are of being loved and nurtured.

No matter how hard conscientious parents try to provide their children with a healthy, loving, supportive upbringing, however, inconsistencies and contradictions in the infant's earliest experiences of life are inevitable. In fact, the very formation of every infant's incipient self-identity depends on an inevitable contradiction: that all of its needs are not immediately met. For example, parents cannot always respond the instant baby is hungry; baby wants to be held and comforted, but the parents want to change its diapers, or put baby to bed, or give it a bath; baby's stomach hurts, and the pain doesn't go away instantly. These and countless other discrepancies and lags between the infant's felt needs, and if, when, and how those needs are met, contribute to an infant's early recognition that it is a "self" separate from its world.

These lags between the infant's needs and their fulfillment are inevitable. No mortal parent could fulfill every need the moment, and precisely to the degree, the infant felt each need. If this were possible, and the infant found that its world instantaneously and perfectly satisfied every one of its needs, the child's sense of self might well never develop. The infant might literally feel at one with its universe.

Nevertheless, this lag also creates insecurity. The infant cannot understand the logic behind its desires not being met: why its hunger does not cease, why it needs to be changed or bathed or put in its crib alone, why it is not consistently held and comforted. The infant cannot understand the logic behind this duality between itself and its world. This duality not only contributes to the infant's sense of self, but simultaneously implies uncertainty, insecurity, aloneness, separateness. This duality assures that at the basis of every personality, there lurks a degree of uncertainty, insecurity, anxiety, fear. In the Upanishads there is a saying: *Dvitiyad vai bhayam bhavati,* "Certainly fear is born of duality." At the very basis of the formation of our sense of self is insecurity, fear. None who are born escape it.

In this, we see that our precious sense of individuality, and an uncomfortable sense of alienation from life and grace (grace referring here to having all our needs and desires effortlessly fulfilled), are two sides of the same coin. As we continue to develop, we naturally cherish our individuality, but we also wish to free ourselves from the alienation, uncertainty, and insecurity of duality. We want to live in grace.

Loving, supportive family relationships early in life give us the security of love and help to build a healthy sense of self. Later, close friendships, and successes in school, athletics, and eventually in our careers, all help to further develop a secure self-worth. Failures in these areas, however, touch the nerve of inner uncertainty and insecurity. If we are lucky, we gradually accumulate enough successes to carve out a more or less healthy, positive, assured self-identity. Gradually, the initial impressions of insecurity and uncertainty are forgotten.

Does this amount, then, to finally having healed these impressions of insecurity? Not entirely. This task is still incomplete. Inevitably, this process of development has involved some degree of repression.

Forming the boundaries of our self-identities is a necessary step of growth. Yet boundaries necessarily imply exclusion. We take in some experiences, thoughts, feelings, and perceptions, we build upon those; and we exclude other experiences, thoughts, feelings, and perceptions. No one has everything go perfectly in their lives. We cannot form a positive self-identity if we fully "take in" all of our experiences. Life is too vast. It has too many contradictions, too much potential dissonance. To some degree, nearly everyone represses the intrusion of sexual urges, destructive thoughts, anger, or fear. We also selectively ignore, if not actively repress, the complexity implied by the existence of so many points of view other than our own. We tend to assume that we know what reality is. We fail to fully open ourselves to the actual complexity of life, which would certainly overwhelm us. In the words of the bird in a T. S. Eliot poem, "Human kind cannot bear very much reality."

Uncertainty and insecurity compose the ground in which the seed of human reality germinates. Were we to attempt to take in everything, we would be overwhelmed, tossed and turned in an ocean of uncertainty. Repression is therefore an inevitable and necessary step in human development. The human ego is thus necessarily one-sided and divided to some degree—no matter how ideal one's childhood, no matter how many successes we experience in life.

This, then, is why connecting with the core of our feelings is not so easy—why, in fact, it is so very rare. Our lives are castles built on sand. To enter the core of our feelings is to let go of the cherished and secure boundaries upon which our identities rest. This holds the ominous promise of a fall from whatever happiness and security, whatever sense of grace, we have managed to carve out for ourselves. Ultimately, though, we cannot carve a sense of grace in our lives; we can only open our heart to receive grace.

The price we pay by ignoring this, by not opening to our own inner feelings, is untold. Rather than looking to explore and heal the divisions within ourselves, we hope to complete ourselves by forever chasing after any number of outside things: success, love, money, travel, material possessions, self-expression, knowledge, a perfect marriage. Yet none of these ultimately satisfy. So long as we remain divided, we never quite find lasting and complete happiness. As we never become whole, neither do we fully experience life.

This does not mean that we are not capable of acting effectively. We may fulfill many desires, learn many things. Yet complete fulfillment will elude us; for what suffers most is not our ability to act, nor our intellectual ability, but our access to the subtlest, most delicate levels of feeling that connect us most intimately to ourselves, to others, to life, to an experience of intrinsic meaning in our existence. It is on this delicate level of feeling that our relationship with life exists. It is on this level of feeling that we feel either nurtured, supported, in union with life, or alienated, in opposition to life. Without access to the full range of our feelings, life loses its poetry. We cannot feel a depth of joy and peace. Finding success in life is one thing; finding happiness is quite another. To achieve the latter, we must open to, and heal, our hearts.

Intimate, love relationships hold such potential for growth and healing because they so directly challenge us to open to the core of our feelings. When we are separate from ourselves and our own feelings, we cannot sustain true intimacy with another. We cannot give love freely, unconditionally. Instead, we inadvertently act in ways that reinforce our hidden insecurities, fears, and sense of separation. Thus intimate relationships so often seem to create misery for both partners.

As far as our happiness is concerned, it may be far better to remain single if we are not interested in growth and healing, for eventually intimacy will push and pull at the deepest boundaries of our sense of self. We will experience this pushing and pulling as problems, conflicts, irritations—as obstacles to our happiness. Indeed, if we are innocent and open, and if we do not become numb, our relationship will invisibly touch the nerve of our deepest insecurities and fears. An intimate love relationship catches us in an accelerated process perfectly designed to open and heal us.

Our reactions to each other, then, which seem to obstruct our love and happiness, are themselves the pathways to the happiness we seek—if, that is, we learn to use them to explore ourselves, to feel all of our feelings, if we learn to use them to heal the hidden sources of alienation, blindness, and one-sidedness within ourselves. If we do, we will come to know what it means to be a true lover, a true husband, wife, mother, or father. We will feel what it means to be a true human being.

LISTENING TO OUR FEELINGS

*A*s deep as some of our emotional wounds may be, we *can* heal our hearts. Just as listening with compassion and an intention to allow our partner to heal creates a healing chemistry of feeling between us, listening to our own feelings in this way can awaken an inner healing chemistry.

Unfortunately, we rarely do this. Normally, we do not want to feel the feelings that need healing because they are uncomfortable—anger, fear, insecurity, sadness, anxiety, and so on. We tend to ignore them, repress them, go over the top of them, or enter into a subtle tug-of-war with them in the name of "working through" them. We may analyze our feelings, we may wallow in them; but we hardly ever experience our feelings in a way that results in a release and healing.

Our approach to our own feelings parallels the way we approach each other's feelings. We don't like to experience our partner's uncomfortable feelings any more than our own. Thus we may react and force our partner to bottle up their anger; we may ignore or discount their fears and insecurities; we may enter into a tug-of-war to work through our differences by arguing, negotiating, compromising; we may analyze each other's problems and suggest solutions. These tactics usually fail to result in any significant healing of our partner, and they don't work much better in relation to our own feelings. The key to inner healing lies in *attending* to our feelings with care and love and an innocent intention to heal.

Attention is the most fundamental commodity of our lives. Where and how we focus our attention determines what our lives become. If we always direct our attention outward—on our job, on entertainment, even on only being with each other—then we are not taking time to stay connected with our own inner life. By seeking our happiness outside of ourselves, we are not properly attending to the seeker. To find happiness, it is precisely the seeker that must be attended to.

When we attend to our feelings with love and a healing intention, we are not simply wallowing in them. This is one reason many neglect to attend to their feelings: No one wants to get caught in an emotional mire. But this need not be the case. In the experience I recounted in the beginning of this chapter, as my feelings progressed from anger to anxiety, to fear, to anguish, I felt detached curiosity about them. In this state insights also came, as if on their own. Though I was feeling my feelings fully, without reserve, I was not caught up in them but *attending* to them. It was only at the end, when I felt the influx of peace and wholeness, that I fully identified with my feelings, for at that point I was centered in myself.

I did not, however, *try* to witness my feelings. Trying to witness one's thoughts and feelings can help maintain equanimity in the midst of our feelings. It may give us a sense of objectivity if we already are caught in an emotional mire. As a form of meditation, it may bring greater discrimination. Nevertheless, it does not directly cultivate the sensitivity and subtlety to explore, heal, and free the deepest, most delicate levels of our heart. If we embrace our feelings, however, we will open our heart.

Attending to our feelings, with an innocent healing intention, creates a chemistry of inner vulnerability. In effect, by embracing uncomfortable feelings with a healing intention, we lift a boundary that we normally place between ourselves and the whole of our being. Instead of overlooking, denying, or repressing our feelings, we allow ourselves to feel, release, and heal them. To open to our feelings in this way is to open our heart to life.

Most of us would rather focus on the positive than attend to what needs healing within us. Positive thinking, focusing on the good in our lives, using techniques of creative visualization and affirmations, all these can be important, even vital aids in healing and life enrichment. Yet when a positive approach entails repressing or denying feelings, we will be thwarting our own healing. As Carl

Jung put it, "One does not become enlightened by imagining figures of light, but by making the darkness conscious."

Thus positive approaches gain much greater value when we are first fully connected with what we are feeling. In fact, attending to one's feelings for the sake of healing is in itself affirming. Our very intention to heal implies that "I am essentially good, healthy, strong, meant to be happy; so let me embrace, release, and heal, and gain meaning from these seemingly negative feelings, and turn them into a process that is profoundly positive." This is a great subconscious affirmation; it can be much deeper and more powerful than a conscious affirmation, which may leave a subconscious sense of low self-esteem untouched.

When we attend to our feelings, we are also spontaneously owning our feelings. We are acknowledging something within us that requires healing. We are not focused on someone else's problem or responsibility.

This overcomes the greatest single obstacle to emotional healing: justifying our reactions by focusing on each other's responsibility, which denies our own responsibility and need for healing. Focusing on each other's problem only feeds our own negative reactions and makes our own healing impossible.

The case of a woman who attended one of my relationship workshops illustrates how subtly we cut ourselves off from our own healing. Joan was in a relationship with a man who could not return her love in the ways she needed. She yearned for the commitment of marriage, and this only pushed him further away. This issue of his unwillingness to commit, and Joan's need for commitment, became the source of almost constant conflict in their relationship. Joan felt nearly continual pain and resentment; the man was frequently in a reaction of emotional withdrawal and anger. Even though she saw how her desperation for commitment was only pushing him away further, Joan felt she could do nothing about it. As she told me emphatically, "This is what I'm feeling and I've got to feel it!"

From her perspective, this meant that she was determined to remain connected to her true feelings. Yet as laudable as her intention might have been, this attitude neither served her own healing nor their relationship. She *demanded* a communion of feeling, not just from love, but from insecurity, pain, and anger. She saw only how his fear was denying both of them the happiness she envisioned. Even though Joan knew that her desperation was a problem, she could not focus on her own need to heal. She blamed her partner for the situation.

Though Joan was apparently connecting with all of her feelings, the way she was connecting prevented healing. This does not mean, however, that if we are reacting, we have no opportunity to heal. We may start off almost completely caught in a negative reaction, but if there is at least the seed of a desire to heal ourselves, it can sprout and bear fruit as we attend to our feelings.

This is what happened to me when I sat with my irritation in the example at the beginning of this chapter. Recognizing that it would serve no purpose to act on my irritation, I closed my eyes to settle down. As my feelings unfolded, I became progressively more aware that my irritation, fear, and anguish were emanating from insecurity within myself. Initially, I had held Susan responsible for my irritation, but I couldn't blame her for my insecurity. Like it or not, at this point I was owning my feelings.

This act is empowering and liberating. It liberates us from our reactions to others. It frees us from our own anger and resentment—feelings that chafe at our hidden inner wounds. This can help heal a relationship, because instead of blaming each other, we are looking within. We need not repress our anger or blame, we can attend to our anger and blame and see where they lead us.

EMOTIONS AND THE BODY

Another fascinating aspect of emotional healing is the relationship between emotions and the body. For example, I clearly felt my anguish as a constriction in my chest. This constriction dissolved as my emotions were released. My chest opened. My body felt permeated with a marked calm, even blissful feeling. There is an indisputable relationship between emotional healing and the body.

We experience emotions in the body. We may feel anxiety as a queasiness in the stomach, sadness as a pressure in the chest, fear as a tightening in the solar plexus. When we attend to our feelings with a healing intention, with eyes closed and in a deeply settled state, we will become aware that background or repressed feelings are also experienced in specific areas of the body.

For years, neurophysiologists have known that chemical messengers called neuropeptides are produced in the brain whenever we think or feel. These neuropeptides pass from one nerve cell to another in a process that appears to be the neurophysiological basis for thought and feeling. More recently, scientists have discovered that this process is active, not only in brain cells, but in many other cells in the body, including the immune cells, cells in the stomach, liver, kidneys, and so on. In other words, the processes underlying thought and feeling, once believed to be exclusively located in the central nervous system, are actually taking place throughout our bodies. As Dr. Deepak Chopra concludes in his tape series *Magical Mind, Magical Body,* we have thinking/feeling bodies. The implications of emotional healing for physical health, then, are vast. As researchers become increasingly interested in the interrelations between emotional and physical health, an entire field of study—psychoneuroimmunology—has emerged. Just as we become caught in patterns of feeling, thinking, and interacting, so our bodies become caught in corresponding patterns of subtle neurophysiological functioning. Just as we come to think that our personal experience is reality, so the health of our bodies reflect that reality—for better or for worse. We can heal our hearts—and in so doing we can heal our bodies.

The relationship between the emotions and the body also helps explain why we cannot rationally think or will ourselves into healing emotionally. If all the hidden layers of our emotional reality are reflected in the body's neuro-physiological functioning, then emotional healing must affect the body in extremely subtle and complex ways. Significant emotional healing will create changes in how the whole body/mind/heart experiences reality.

I may tell myself that, as frustrating as my partner is, he or she is just what I need to grow. That may be entirely true, but thinking that does not prevent my resentment from building. I may genuinely want to forgive my partner for a grievous offense, but I cannot simply shove my anger and resentment aside. I will have to experience an actual shift—physically as well as emotionally—before I am free of all the layers of my reaction. In working with clients, I have observed that emotional healing is inevitably accompanied by an awareness of release and healing in the body. This may be as dramatic as the sudden disappearance of psy-chosomatic ailments, such as ulcers; or it may be as simple as an easing of tension in the shoulders, an opening or freeing of constriction in the chest, or an overall sense of physical relaxation and peace.

This connection between emotions and the body is part of the unique power of a love relationship: We are not only emotionally intimate, but physically intimate as well.

We share the layers of each other's feelings—our joy, love, fears, insecurities—not just emotionally, but even physically. With our feelings, words, and touch, we can nurture and uplift each other on all levels of our being. This is the beauty and responsibility of an intimate relationship.

PRACTICAL STEPS TO HEALING THE HEART*

othing could be more natural than healing the heart. We already have healing power within us. In one way or another, we heal ourselves everyday. We get sick, we rest, we drink plenty of fluids, and we get well. We cut ourselves, and the body heals. Every day we get tired, we sleep at night, and the next day we wake up fresh, rejuvenated; this is a healing. Even more dramatically, every year hundreds of cases of terminal illness are inexplicably reversed. How? Medical science has no idea. Somehow these people activate the healing power within themselves.

Every cell in our bodies—in fact, every living cell, in even the simplest organisms—is equipped with enzymatic processes to heal itself. Healing is a part of life.

Likewise, emotions also tend to heal naturally. The first time you were left by a girlfriend or boyfriend for

*Individuals with a history of emotional instability or mental illness, or those in emotional crises, should seek the advice of a competent professional before following the suggestions of this chapter. Inner healing as described in this chapter is not meant to replace therapy or psychiatric treatment.

someone else, perhaps you thought you'd never recover, but you did. In a quiet moment, you may remember back to that relationship and feel how you have deepened as a result of both the relationship and the loss of the relationship. Healing permeates life. If we can simply come out of our distorted patterns of denial and repression, if we can open to our own hearts, life begins to heal us as naturally as a night's sleep refreshes us.

In fact, emotional healing is so simple and natural that at some time or another, everyone has experienced it. Perhaps it happens as a result of a good cry, or even from being profoundly moved by an affecting movie. (It's safe to experience our emotions in a movie, and so we may well come out of one feeling renewed, more alive.) Unfortunately, many of us rarely take the time to explore all the layers of our feelings. We get so absorbed in routines of daily life that we lose connection with ourselves, and with life's natural healing power. This is like working day and night without taking time to sleep. No wonder we have trouble communicating!

To heal our hearts, we do not have to adopt an entirely new lifestyle, however. We need only take the opportunities to heal as they arise. If an issue comes up in our relationship, and we react, that is a chance to heal. If we simply feel a vague sense of uneasiness, unhappiness, or irritability, for whatever reason, that is a time to heal. Perhaps we feel pressured at work, irritated with a co-worker, worried about money, or just become disconnected from ourselves by keeping a hectic pace. Anytime we feel something other than a sense of balance, centeredness, peace, and joy, that is an open door to the core of our feelings.

Sometimes even positive feelings may open that door. We may, for instance, feel thrilled about getting something we have really wanted. Yet lasting happiness does not come from external things. Our high is sure to end. We can enjoy our achievements; but by following our excitement to its hidden sources, we may heal ourselves of whatever lack we were seeking to fill in ourselves. Then we may enjoy our achievements from a state of balance and centeredness.

When you feel the need for healing, go to a private place where you will not be disturbed. Sit quietly and close your eyes. Because healing involves physiological as well as emotional and psychological shifts, it requires energy. Our emotional, mental, and physical resources should not be otherwise engaged. A restful state, ideally a deep, meditative state, is best.

With eyes closed, first simply feel what comes. For example, if you have been in an argument, feel your anger or defensiveness. Be with these feelings. As you do so, notice any corresponding tightness, constriction, pressure, or uneasiness in your body. In other words, be sensitive to where the feelings seem to be coming from in your body. Once the emotional sensation and the physical sensation become clearly related, open to them more actively. You may experience a sense of leaning into them, embracing them, or going into the heart of them.

Embracing our feelings in this way lifts the boundaries we normally place between ourselves and uncomfortable feelings—boundaries that hold emotional and physical patterns in place, inhibiting the body's natural healing ability. By embracing our feelings with a healing intention, in a deeply restful state, these boundaries can dissolve. This allows for a natural release and healing, orchestrated with wonderful efficiency by the body's innate healing intelligence. Though it may require more time in some cases, I have often seen a client's mood of depression or anger, which may have been dragging on for days, completely dissolve in a matter of minutes as a result of this exercise.

Emotional healing need not involve great emotive release. I frequently work with clients who know they have a lot of anger or sadness. Before beginning their first healing session with me, some expect to do a lot of yelling or crying. One client even warned me, "I know I have a lot of anger, so I'll probably do some yelling once we start. And, uh, do you happen to have a pillow I could hit?" He was more than a little disappointed when I told him it wouldn't be necessary.

This man was expecting to release immediate feelings of anger in the way he had learned to in the past—even though he acknowledged those ways had not cooled his fiery temper. True emotional healing takes place at levels of feeling deeper and more subtle than ordinary emotion. These "seed levels" of feeling, from which ordinary emotions spring, are the hidden, underlying patterns of feeling, formed by our life experiences. They respond to cues within our present circumstances to evoke feelings and reactions. Sometimes emotive release is a part of healing these seed feelings, as when Susan experienced a healing of the sorrow from her mother's death. At other times dramatic release is not necessary for deep healing. In healing my hidden anguish and insecurity, tears did not come at all. The difference depends not only on the person and the feeling that is being healed, but also on the circumstance and method of healing. The emotional healing described in this chapter tends to be a gentle, subtle experience analogous to meditation, only on the level of feeling, not thinking.

This raises another point. Although thoughts will inevitably come during the process, they need not distract us. We can let them go as they come, by simply, gently bringing our awareness back to our feeling. Healing is not a mental process, but a visceral one. Even if insights come, they are the by-product of the process of healing, not the cause. Therefore, we need not try to analyze thoughts or dwell on their content. Insight will help to integrate our healing, but we can contemplate our insights afterward.

The emphasis on the healing process as visceral rather than mental is significant. If I am feeling anger and I dwell on the thoughts that come, I may find myself turning over and over in my mind the circumstances relating to my anger: the sequence of events, who was at fault, the innumerable character flaws of the irritating person. (This last point of meditation alone might keep me busy fuming for hours.) In other words, I would be wallowing in my anger, not healing it.

If, however, I leave the thoughts and simply feel the emotion of anger, my anger will soon dissolve, or even transform into a different feeling altogether. This is just what happened to my irritation with Susan. It first dissolved into fear, then anguish, then insecurity, and finally into bliss and caring for her. Anger is never the bottom line. We are angry because we have been hurt, are afraid, or feel threatened or insecure. To heal the anger, we need to transcend the anger and connect with the core of our feelings.

This holds true of any emotion. If we dwell on the content of the thoughts that come, we will not be healing but wallowing, whether they be sad, angry, or fearful thoughts. By not minding the content of our thoughts, we can heal in minutes viscerally what might take days of struggling to resolve on the level of thinking.

Again we see a parallel between healing communication and inner healing. Just as we benefit by waiting to work out the practical details of a situation until we are free from our reactions, until we feel a communion, so we benefit by waiting to consider the content of thoughts until our self-healing is completed. Trying to resolve an issue of conflict with each other can consume hours or even days of arguing and hard feelings; but it can come gracefully once we have communicated in a way that allows us to feel our hearts touching. Likewise, we can consume days privately mulling over our thoughts, hoping to analyze and work through our feelings; yet if we put aside thoughts and follow our feelings to their core, our thoughts will be transformed.

In other words, even personal meaning and insight come much more readily in a visceral process. As we connect with the core of our feelings, we experience a tangible shift—emotionally, physically, mentally. Our whole reality changes. From this new reality we spontaneously see things in a more personal and meaningful light. We don't need to struggle for insight or meaning. We don't need to analyze ourselves or the situation. Analyzing ourselves for insight, or struggling with ourselves to feel positive emotions such as forgiveness, love, understanding, is far less efficient. It is like wearing dark glasses and straining to imagine what the world looks like without them. As we follow our feelings to our core, we find that the glasses simply fall off, and we see the world clearly.

It may happen that an emotion comes that seems too strong or frightening, or perhaps you feel lost in it. In that case, let your awareness be with only the physical dimension of the feeling without minding your emotions. That is, let your awareness simply caress any physical sensation that seems to be related to the emotion. This will have a soothing effect emotionally, yet still facilitate healing in a more gentle, gradual way. When you feel more comfortable, you may either conclude or continue.

You can also adopt a loving, caring attitude toward your own feelings and their associated physical sensations. For instance, if you feel anxiety and tightness in your stomach, you can caress those feelings with a caring, soothing awareness. This may be particularly appropriate if you feel overshadowed by your emotions, or feel no center (that is, no sense of *attending* to the feelings).

At some point your feelings may turn, and you will find yourself experiencing a sense of release, expansion, peace, or connectedness with self. If this happens, continue to sit with your eyes closed, and take a few minutes to enjoy the benefits of the healing that has just taken place. This is also a good time to enjoy any insight, or sense of personal meaning gained (without trying to do so).

Sometimes you may feel that nothing is happening, and begin to feel frustrated or restless. But something *is* happening: You are feeling frustrated or restless. Even this can be an open door to some underlying blocked emotion. Embrace the restlessness and frustration.

Sometimes you will be with a feeling that does not move significantly in one sitting or even in three or four sittings. Still, you are connecting with yourself, and even this will be centering and balancing. Eventually, it will start to move and open. In the meantime, you are coming into a new, conscious relationship with the core of your feelings. You are owning them, they are not owning and buffeting you. You are living more authentically—connected with yourself.

If you feel you want to pray or meditate during the process, you may, but very gently, effortlessly, without disconnecting from your emotions. If prayer or meditation is motivated by a desire to have a good or "spiritual" experience, however, it can lead to repressing feelings that need healing. Prayer or meditation can certainly add healing power, provided you remain connected to your feelings. Offering your pain to God may also add a devotional dimension to your healing, and deepen your sense of a personal relationship with God. Nevertheless, though potentially complementary to the healing process, prayer and meditation are not requisites to healing. Neither is emotional healing intended to replace prayer, meditation, or other spiritual practices. These have their own unique value.

Sometimes the process will seem complete in a few minutes, sometimes healing may come in waves for a longer time. After ten minutes or so, even if you feel no release or healing, you should end the session with the awareness that many emotional wounds require more time to heal. Approach healing with patience. Don't expect giant daily breakthroughs; healing the heart is a lifelong journey. That journey becomes all the more joyful and balanced if we approach it with patience, loving ourselves enough to accept the process of healing and growth as it naturally unfolds.

When you end a session of inner healing, it is important to allow your body and emotions to settle fully before you return to activity. Lie down on your back with your eyes closed, relaxed in your body and mind, and rest for at least as much time as you spent sitting with your feelings. If you feel physical sensations at this time, you may innocently allow your awareness to caress those sensations, without dwelling on any residual emotions that may come. With this attitude, you may spontaneously begin to witness your thoughts and feelings. If any uncomfortable emotion remains after your session, do not attempt to continue to "be with it" during your day's activity. Such efforts more often result in wallowing in an uncomfortable feeling, rather than in healing it. The effectiveness of your activity is also likely to suffer. Again, healing takes place most efficiently when we give our feelings total attention in a restful state. Once a session is over, forget about healing. Engage fully in your activity—the more dynamically the better if there is any lingering emotional discomfort. This will be integrating, and will allow you to enjoy the benefits of the healing that has taken place.

Finally, healing in the context of a relationship means not only healing yourself, but expressing the benefits within the relationship. When the session is over, seek out your partner and forgive, apologize, or express any new-found appreciation in some way. Expressing what you have gained is vital to integrating your healing. If, after connecting with your feelings, you still do not feel your love, then at least you will be better prepared to communicate.

One way to express our caring for each other is to give each other time for healing. Poet Rainer Maria Rilke once wrote: "A good marriage is that in which each appoints the other guardian of his solitude." Here is a chance to do just that. If you see that your partner is upset, agitated, or down, ask if they would like to have some time alone. Offer to take over whatever they are doing and give them that time. We know we are successfully attending to our own feelings when we find ourselves attending to the feelings of each other.

CHAPTER FIVE

THE WAY OF GIVING
Expressing Our Love Through Action

As we grow together on the path of love, we gradually recreate both our individual realities and the reality of our relationship. Going beyond our anger and healing our hearts, learning to consciously receive each other, are inward aspects of this process. They open our heart to *feel* love. But we must not only feel love, we must express it. Only as we express love are we truly recreated.

We can express love in three basic ways: silently, with words, and through action. Our silent expressions of love—a touch, a hug, a look—are often the deepest. At some moments anything more would seem clumsy and inappropriate, and would bring us out of that depth of love. Nonverbal expressions of love, when deeply heartfelt, usually mark the greatest vulnerability, openness, and stillness—and result in a deep sense of union.

Human beings, however, are not by nature silent. We speak, we sing, we laugh, and we hear each other. We even think in terms of language. To feel a complete relationship with each other, we need not only to feel our love, but to speak of our love; we need not only to feel that we are loved, but to hear that we are loved. This creates and maintains a sense of intimacy. Words do more than simply express our love, they stir and enliven it.

Finally, we can express love by actively giving to each other. Most of our waking life is spent in action, and our love must naturally extend into our actions. This is what we normally think of as giving: going out of our way to help, support, nurture, or show attention through some form of action. Many of our routine tasks of living together and maintaining a household can also become giving, when done in a spirit of service and love. It may be as simple as sacrificing a favorite TV show to be with your partner, putting the cap back on the toothpaste, hanging up your partner's clothes when they fall off the hanger, making a special meal, suggesting a vacation day together, bringing home a thoughtful gift, and so on.

A healthy relationship implies a balance between all these expressions of love. Giving love through action, however, has a special significance for the giver. Because giving through action is the most concrete, here is where we most feel the benefits of being recreated by love. To act from love requires more effort than to feel love, or to speak of our love. Action involves more of our being. Action channels our feelings from our heart, through our mind, through our personality and character, and right into our bodies.

We can talk of love, write of love, gaze into each other's eyes, and yet remain self-centered and self-indulgent. Giving through action involves a sacrifice of time, energy, and attention that is above and beyond that involved in nonverbal and verbal expressions of love. Giving through action is not only a sign that we enjoy feeling affection for each other, but of our awareness, sensitivity, and selflessness. For this reason nothing integrates love into our lives more powerfully than expressing our caring through action. Active giving brings the hidden beauty of love to transform our outer daily lives.

Giving, then, is a great key to realizing the promise of the heart. Nevertheless, the natural demands in a relationship to give may press us right up against our inner boundaries. Giving may seem to involve a difficult personal sacrifice of energy and attention, or rub against ingrained ideas of fairness and equality: What if my partner does not give in return? Will I be taken advantage of? Will my giving be taken for granted? Instead of being the means to our fulfillment, giving may seem an obstacle to our happiness.

Dangers also lurk in trying too hard. The person who makes heroic efforts to give selflessly may end up stuffing resentment that later oozes out and eats at the relationship like acid. It is easy to speak of the virtues of giving, but we are not perfect human beings. We have little hope of learning to give gracefully, freely, if we simply keep telling ourselves how we *should be*. Such thinking makes selfless giving an unattainable ideal, not an organic experience.

But this ideal, extolled by all the great spiritual traditions of the world, need not be unattainable. It need not require constant inner struggle. If we are patient with ourselves as well as each other, we can gradually experience a shift in awareness that will suffuse our actions with a graceful, generous love.

THE ESSENCE OF GIVING

*I*n our age of prenuptial agreements, negotiated compromises, women's rights, men's rights—an age in which a premium is often placed on self-assertion and "getting what's coming to us"—the value of giving has been subtly eclipsed. For many, the word "giving" in an intimate relationship has come to evoke any number of negative images: "self-sacrificing," "martyrdom," "codependency."

Ironically, this virtue has fallen from popularity because for too long, too many people have striven to live up to it. Straining to give, trying to be "good," trying to live up to any ideal that is not an organic expression of our feelings, inevitably accents the opposite of that ideal within us. I have seen many well-meaning wives who have given and given in their marriages to self-centered husbands. By the time they come for counseling, they are seething with resentment, and their self-absorbed husbands appear to be innocent victims. Equally unfortunate is the person who gives and gives to an unappreciative partner, only to end up feeling the martyr.

Our intention to live our ideals opens the door to growth. Yet, that same intention will eventually underscore the hidden imbalances and wounds we need to heal within ourselves. It is only as we heal that we become one with ourselves, whole and freely loving. Then our ideals cease to be ideals and become natural, integrated expressions of ourselves. This healing can never happen, however, as long as we deny that we are wounded, as long as we simply strain to give. When we fail to embrace what needs to be healed within ourselves, our ideals remain ever out of our reach, and we will experience them as struggle.

This struggle is reflected in the commonplace conception of giving. We generally think of giving as going out of our way to do something for someone else. We might define it as "an expenditure of energy, time, and effort made for the benefit of another." This is one aspect of giving, but it is not the essence of giving. It is the way we see giving so long as we are not one with ourselves.

Giving, at least in the context of a love relationship, means much more than this. I define giving as *an expression of love through action, intended to serve the happiness and well-being of the beloved.* Though this definition appears similar to the one given above, there is one vast difference: love.

This is the essence of giving. When my action is an expression of my caring, it is not a strain. It is a natural expression of my organic experience and feelings, and it transforms my experience of giving. Not only does the person I give to receive the benefits of my actions, but I also receive joy and energy from them. I am uplifted. I feel myself recreated by my actions. An act done without a lively feeling of caring is simply an expenditure of energy. A robot can be programmed to do almost any action. Human beings can perform actions with love, whereby they gain energy. Human beings can give.

It is true that this definition of giving includes the idea of doing something for someone else—"the intention to serve the happiness and well-being of another"—but this intention is an expression of love. Not just love that we "know" we feel, or sometimes feel, or should feel, but *do* feel, in the moment of giving. When we care for someone, we naturally desire their happiness. It can be a joy to make your partner a special dinner when you are feeling a lively appreciation for them. It will be a headache to do it when you don't feel that appreciation. Straining to give to your partner day after day is a formula for martyrdom and migraines, not love.

I have counseled couples who found this a difficult concept to accept. They insisted that giving when we *don't* feel our love is real giving, that this is going the extra mile. Well, they are right in one respect: They will have to go an extra mile to get around the walls of resentment they will be building if they continue to give without feeling their love.

Struggling and straining to give is not only a neglect of ourselves and our true feelings, but a neglect of the relationship. We are going through the motions of love without feeling it. Imagine gazing into each other's eyes, but without feeling. Such a look might be positively frightening. Enough looks like that might end a relationship. Imagine your partner reciting words of love, while conveying only irritation that you felt the need to hear them. Those words will ring hollow and untrue. They will not stir affection, but distrust and insecurity in return. Yet somehow we have come to accept that actions done without a living, breathing feeling may still be called expressions of our love. It simply is not true. This, too, endangers the relationship.

In an intimate relationship, it is not just the thought that counts, it is the feeling. "Giving" without feeling will not advance the relationship on the path of love even one inch. Instead, this is one of the great dead-end trails leading off the path of love. It is lined with road signs like, "Next Rest Area 1,000 Miles" and "Caution, Falling Resentment." Indeed, this dead-end trail has become a major highway through so much use. At the end of this highway are mountains made of the wreckage of countless relationships.

BECOMING MORE GIVING MEANS BECOMING MORE LOVING

Becoming more giving means becoming more loving. I did not really understand this until a relatively minor incident forever changed my perspective. On this particular night, I was scheduled to give Susan a massage.

Susan is a massage therapist who happens to love receiving massages. Several years before, she had taught me how to give a more or less adequate one, so that we could take turns massaging each other. The problem was that Susan *liked* giving them; and although I liked *receiving* massages, when it came to giving them, I'd rather do almost anything else. In fact, kneading someone who doesn't even want to make conversation, who just wants to soak it up, and who expects not a ten- or fifteen-minute token rubdown, but an hour-long, full-body, therapist-quality massage, was for me truly a trial.

As the hour of our rendezvous approached, the low energy and tired feeling I had been experiencing that day advanced into body aches and what felt like a slight fever. I carefully took stock of my symptoms; no, I was not imagining this, I was coming down with the flu. I went to find Susan and let her know that I would not be able to give the massage, but before I could say anything she hugged me and told me how much she was looking forward to it. With a moan, I told her that I was not feeling too well and warned her that I might have to cut it short.

As I began the massage following dinner, I was feverish, and my body ached. I had a sore throat and the beginnings of a headache. I braced myself with the knowledge that I would surely cut the massage down to half an hour or so. As I began kneading her feet, she moaned in relief. They had been killing her. Same with her legs. I continued massaging. Again, she sighed with relief when I got to her back. Every inch of her body seemed to need and invite caring and healing. By the time I got to her shoulders, instead of counting the minutes, I found myself thinking about how hard she worked—massaging others, cleaning, cooking, giving to me and our girls—and the effects of all this on her body. Maybe it was because I was expecting the worst from being sick, or maybe it was grace—or maybe I was just delirious from fever—but I felt a wave of compassion for Susan. I found myself wanting only to give her a wonderful massage.

For the rest of the session, I was oblivious to the time. For the most part I forgot that I was sick. I felt absorbed in making Susan feel better. I felt completely in the present, focused only on giving to her—my hands seemed imbued with a massage magic of their own. Well over an hour later we finished. I left her to relax on the massage table and silently left the room.

I admit, I was pleased with myself. Here I had really given, in a sustained way, for over an hour, while sick. It was a first for me. Now I looked forward to a well-deserved night's sleep. I went into the kitchen to get a glass of water, and my heart sank at the sight that greeted me. There were all the dishes and pans from two previous meals—unwashed, unrinsed, caked with food. The place was a disaster. I would have left the whole mess until the next morning, but from experience I knew that Susan would never let it go overnight. All would have to be done before bed. Once again, I felt overwhelmed by body aches and tiredness; I wanted only to crawl into bed. Still, I didn't want Susan to have to do this cleaning after the massage. I knew she would just want to relax in bed. I decided to do it myself, and if possible, to have it all done before she came out of the massage room.

I dove into the task. Miraculously, just as before, literally every moment I was cleaning, every motion of scrubbing, rinsing, drying, was filled with an awareness of giving for Susan's happiness. My sickness became just a fact, a part of the situation. It did not keep me from feeling the warmth of love. I actually enjoyed every minute of cleaning the kitchen.

By the time Susan emerged, I was just finishing the kitchen. She thanked me profusely for the massage and for cleaning up, but quite honestly, that made little difference. In fact, I remember having the rather surprising wish that Susan would not even notice, that she would say nothing about the massage or the kitchen. I wanted to remain as anonymous as possible; I had already received so much, there was no need for any acknowledgment.

Whereas the massage began as an endurance test, a struggle to "do something for someone else," the moment I began to receive Susan, feel my appreciation for all that she gives in her life, the massage became giving. It became an expression of caring that energized and healed my whole being. There is no doubt in my mind that I received much more that evening than Susan did. She received a loving massage; I received a glimpse of my higher self, my creative, loving humanness.

GIVING CONSCIOUSNESS

*N*ormally, the issue of giving in a relationship raises any number of concerns: How do I give without being taken advantage of? Where should I draw the line? How do we establish a healthy balance of giving and receiving in our relationship? As extreme as it may sound, it is only as we lose touch with the essence of giving that such questions enter our minds.

Giving is inherently fulfilling. It is the most concrete expression of love. When we are in the experience of true giving, we do not care whether or not the giving is returned. We do not want to draw the line anywhere. We would give without limits if at all possible, because the experience of giving is entirely blissful, expansive, and grace-filled. Anyone the least interested in personal or spiritual growth, or even in becoming happy, who ever has a pure experience of giving, will want nothing more than to have more of that experience. They would give anything for it.

I am speaking of a state of consciousness in which we are actually experiencing action as an expression of love. The night of that massage, for instance, each moment that I was giving, I would not have chosen to be anywhere else or do anything else. I would not have traded places with Susan. I did not want Susan to return my giving. I did not even want her to acknowledge it. Fairness was the furthest thing from my mind. Giving the massage, cleaning the kitchen, were the most blissfully fulfilling experiences I could imagine in that moment. I tangibly felt love flowing through me, through my mind, personality, and body into my actions. I tangibly felt myself being recreated by love.

I was now in an entirely different state of mind than I was in when I first entered the massage room. Then, I was far from the experience of giving, far from the reality of love. As a result, the question of drawing the line was paramount. I had already drawn it—at half an hour. Later that night I also experienced a fall from giving consciousness: when I left the massage room. I stopped giving and began to congratulate myself. I became filled with myself instead of with love. As a result, when I saw the dishes piled up, I responded as I usually had in the past when faced with sacrificing time and energy, seemingly for Susan's benefit: with inertia and reluctance. Once I reentered giving consciousness, the inertia dissolved, and I was again caught in the grace of giving.

Giving is fulfilling because when we give we are filled with so much more light and love than when we are stuck in a mundane attachment to our own comforts and needs. It is no wonder that God is said to be love; for when we allow love to give through us, we tangibly experience grace.

The Way of Giving

That grace also entails a natural sensitivity and humility, such that one wants no recognition or thanks. This feeling is part of the grace that comes with real giving. It is only later, when we are out of that experience of grace, that we might want recognition or thanks.

There is, however, a great danger in speaking of giving in this way. The moment we begin to speak of the virtues of giving, we realize we should be more giving in our relationships. So what do we do? We try to be more giving by *doing more.* An intention to give by doing more for each other is fine, but that intention, if it is ever to expand our giving, must first pass through our love.

When a plant becomes dry, the natural first step is to water the roots. When we realize our efforts to give are dry, when we feel inner resistance or resentment about giving, the obvious remedy is to tend to our feelings for each other. Only after we have nourished our feelings will we be capable of real giving.

Just as when we do not feel love we should not say, "I love you," when we feel a persistent resistance to giving we should not give. We need first to reconnect with our love, whatever it takes, so that we can again give. We water the roots of our relationship so that we can increasingly live in the consciousness of giving.

Since the night I gave Susan that massage, I have caught myself giving without being filled, or giving because I thought I should give, many times. Countless times I have also felt inner resistance to giving and have not even attempted to give. Such experiences are inevitable as we are growing (or, as it may seem, not growing) on the path of love. When we find ourselves unable to give, we can tend to our love in a number of ways. Three of the most important of those ways are through receiving each other, healing the heart, and communicating. In chapter 7 we will explore a fourth way that transcends even these in its power to make love unconditional.

Receiving Each Other

When I began massaging Susan, I felt incapable of giving. Then I suddenly began to receive Susan—I began to appreciate how much of Susan's life is dedicated to helping and caring for myself and others. In this case I did not make an effort to receive her, it happened spontaneously. At other times, however, I have consciously focused on receiving Susan, and this has often allowed me to give to her.

Consciously opening to receive each other is actually one of the simplest ways to tend to our love. I find that it is especially appropriate when there is no obvious problem in our relationship, but for some reason we are not feeling our appreciation for each other. Perhaps we are so absorbed in the demands of our daily lives that we have lost touch with our appreciation. At such times, focusing on the other person's higher qualities can be enough to help us reconnect with our love. Sometimes, to further nurture our appreciation, we may need to take a break from our responsibilities and spend time alone together. Once we feel our love again, we need only put our feelings into action.

Healing the Heart

Sometimes, however, simply intending to receive our partner will not be enough to revive our caring. If we feel hurt, angry, irritated, jealous, we will not be able to give until we have somehow healed these feelings. Trying to receive the other person when caught in such reactions amounts to repression. It won't work. We somehow need to heal these reactions that are strangling our ability to give.

Healing our heart is essential to giving. Healing our reactions heals the divisions within us, so that we give as loving, complete, whole human beings. There is no substitute. Sometimes we can accomplish this by attending to our feelings, as described in the previous chapter. Sometimes it takes a combination of attending to our feelings and focusing on receiving. Then again, sometimes even this is not enough.

Communicating

Communication is the most important way we tend to our love as a couple. Often we cannot heal our hearts alone; we need to express what we are feeling and be heard. In the cause of freeing our love, it is well worth the effort. Communicating when we need to, especially when we do so to free our love and have taken the time to first explore our feelings alone, is tending to our love.

One particular task of communicating that often arises in relation to giving is asking for help. It is difficult to give when you are the one in desperate need of help and you're not getting it. In some relationships, this is not a problem; both partners are in the habit of helping and supporting each other. In my experience, however, such a relationship is the exception. For many couples, asking for help when needed represents a tremendous feat of vulnerability. We may find ourselves nagging, complaining, and arguing in an effort to get the help we need. Or we may find ourselves waiting, hinting, and hoping instead of asking. Even the slightest negativity in a relationship can make asking for help feel like walking over Niagara Falls on a tightrope.

Couples take two common approaches when asking each other for help. Both can lead to disaster.

The first approach is to ask for help as a way to create a more equitable distribution of work in the relationship— whether in general, or just in a given moment: "I've washed the dishes every night this week, now it's your turn." When we ask with this motivation, we are not connected with our love. Rather, we have our accountant's hat on, and are tallying hours spent around the house.

I may well be feeling the pressure of actual imbalance in the relationship, but my reaction to this imbalance will muddy the waters of my asking. Even if I do my best to ask nicely, my partner will, at least subconsciously, pick up that my asking is not coming from a place of appreciation for what they do give. This will almost surely create some resistance.

Again, we communicate feeling with every thought, word, and action. When we ask for help without a sense of appreciation for our partner, we project a reality in which giving is a grudging expenditure of energy, in which our partner has not done enough, in which fairness counts more than feeling and growth. Because feelings tend to be reciprocal, that reality will be reflected back to us—unless our partner can somehow rise above the reality we put out and instead come back with the reality of love.

Indeed, that is exactly what we want our partner to do. We do not want our reality reflected back to us. We do not want an accountant for a partner, a person who helps only to the point of fairness and then shuts off the support. We do not want an irritated or resentful partner. We want the help and support of a loving partner. Yet when we ask for help while disconnected from our appreciation, we will rarely, if ever, get what we really want. We may get a body pitching in, we may get a partner helping just to avoid an argument or the silent resentment treatment, but we are not likely to receive the support of a caring partner. To get the support of a loving partner, somehow we need to *ask* as a loving partner.

Asking with appreciation for our partner may seem to require too much—especially when we feel we are doing a disproportionate share of the "giving." Ultimately, it doesn't matter how unfair things are. That consideration only exists in a universe wherein reality is fixed, and love is only one element balanced by many other factors. The path of love is a universe of a different sort. It is *the* universe, wherein love is the ground state of many realities. Love is reality, but our personal reality shifts according to gradations of the love we experience. One strong probability in this universe is that the way to get loving help and support is to ask with an appreciation of the other person.

This is not to imply that we can repress our irritation and perceptions of unfairness and contrive appreciation. That won't be asking with appreciation. That will be asking with repressed irritation, a perception of unfairness, and a strained attempt at a loving request. Before asking, we can first tend to our love by spending a few moments focusing on receiving. If that doesn't allow us to feel some appreciation, and we have the time, we can tend to our feelings. If that doesn't do it, then we need to raise the issues that are bothering us, we need to communicate to renew our communion. In other words, asking for help, like giving, means first tending to our love. Then when we ask, we will ask as a vulnerable human being who needs the help and support of a caring partner.

The second mistake couples commonly make in asking for help is feeling timid about asking, usually either out of a subconscious fear of creating conflict or a fear of being rejected. No one likes to hear, "No, I'm too busy to help you." This hurts, because it is a rejection of your needs as a person and a negation of your love as a couple. Yet as we have seen, when we act out of our insecurities or fears, we tend to create precisely the reality of which we are most afraid. We project a reality that gets reflected back to us. It doesn't matter if we are asking for help, or not asking for help, or hinting for help, or trying to set an example to get help, or asking in a roundabout way for help. The other person will feel the insecurity or fear within such an effort, and become irritated.

Such an approach is irritating because the asking or hinting is indirect and so comes off as either manipulative, controlling, emotionally needy, or condescending. As a result, their response is likely to be anything but caring help and support. Presto! The button of our insecurity and fear of rejection gets pushed again.

Instead of putting ourselves through all this, we need to face what we are feeling and connect with our insecurities and fears, so that we are not plagued by these feelings. We need to ask from our integrity as a human being deserving of receiving love, and as a person who appreciates the beauty, uniqueness, and giving of their partner. Again, this will probably mean healing our heart or taking the time to come to a communion of feeling through communication.

We deserve to receive each other's support, and we can recognize that asking for that support may be a necessary clearing of the path of our love. Asking for the support we need also clears the path to our giving. We are not just asking for ourselves, we are asking for the relationship.

Sometimes what we need to communicate in order to tend to our love has nothing to do with needing help. Maybe we feel hurt by something that was said, or by something that was done, or left undone. No matter what the specific issue that needs communicating, remember that the goal of communication is a communion of feeling first, and specific details second. With this in mind, we will stand a much greater chance of freeing our love to give.

BRINGING GIVING INTO OUR DAILY LIVES

*O*nce we understand that giving is essentially a state of consciousness in which action becomes an expression of love, an exciting possibility presents itself: to expand conscious giving by bringing it into more and more of our daily routine.

Becoming more giving does not mean that we have to add to our already hectic routines many more thoughtful acts of giving. Hopefully, we can add a few. This will happen naturally as we grow in the consciousness of giving. Yet there is only so much time in a day. If it were just a matter of doing more and more for each other, that would make being recreated by love a practical impossibility. Who has the time? Far more important to growing in our ability to love is to bring our caring and a sense of service into our present actions.

This is not an impossible task. It is a matter of awareness. We need only have an innocent, unstrained intention that all our actions—routine as well as those above and beyond the call of duty—pass through our love for each other.

So often, we lose touch with our love and perform our responsibilities mechanically or from motivations far removed from a sense of service. Instead, we can fulfill the same responsibilities with a consciousness of giving, and create a chemistry of feeling that does give to each other. Even routine actions—earning a living, cooking, cleaning, yard work, laundry—become a means for the growth of giving. We also become softer, more balanced, deeper by acting with an awareness of service. Routine actions become meaningful, joyful; whereas they may have otherwise been driven, trying, resentful, or empty.

This simple shift in intention can make a vast difference in our lives. I could have given the entire massage that night to Susan merely as an obligation. Had I continued to massage Susan as if it were a trial by fire, or even mechanically, she would have noticed my attitude and instead of feeling gratitude, she might well have felt irritated. I know, because it's happened. When we act out of expectation, routine, or for reasons other than to serve each other's well-being and happiness, then we miss out on the benefit of giving. So does our partner.

The most common complaint of modern couples is that they simply have no time for their relationship. Yet, almost magically, the intention to bring giving consciousness into our daily routines creates more time to spend together personally.

There was a time in my life when I was so busy with my career that I barely had five minutes to spend with

Susan each day. The few hours I was at home were dedicated to tending the yard, the car, and the garage, or giving some token attention to the kids. At the time, everything I was doing seemed totally necessary. In retrospect, however, I see those days quite differently. The pressure of the job wasn't all that kept me on a heart attack schedule. I cooperated with those pressures. My life was out of hand because my motivations for success had replaced my consciousness of giving to my family. In a word, I created the imbalance in my life.

Many times I could have chosen to go home rather than keep working, and I gave in to my desire to get ahead at work. Then, when I finally did get home—stressed out, exhausted, wanting only to relax—I often escaped to the relative peace and quiet of working around the house, instead of being with Susan or the kids. I had been disconnected from my love all day. It simply seemed like too great an effort to switch gears and give love that I did not feel.

This is a great secret: When we go through a busy day disconnected from our love, it requires an actual shift in consciousness to begin to give to each other. When a person is already exhausted, this shift in consciousness appears to demand so much as to seem not to be worth the effort. Even giving attention to each other can seem next to impossible. It is so much easier to escape to the TV or to the newspaper.

Yet, if we maintain our awareness of serving each other during the day, no matter how busy we are, no great shift in consciousness is required in the evening. We are tired, but we can still be together. We can still love each other, even if it's only for half an hour before we go to sleep. It is the shift in consciousness that makes giving love such an effort, not simply fatigue. Young lovers can stay up all night together for days on end. They can be physically, mentally, and sexually exhausted, yet feel love in each other's arms with no effort. They do not have to shift consciousness. When love is a backdrop to the entire day, neither do we.

When we act with love, no matter what our apparent responsibilities, our lives tend to stay in perspective. We tend to remain balanced. Actually, it doesn't matter if the love is directed toward each other, toward a child, or toward God. There is a softening, a relaxing, that is incompatible with the hard edges of a driven, imbalanced approach to life. When our caring becomes a silent backdrop to whatever we are doing, the unnecessary and the compulsive fall away. Miraculously, we will find the time to connect with each other. That becomes a priority in our lives.

THE INTENTION TO GIVE

*A*s much as giving is an expression of love, and cannot be forced, giving still requires us to make some effort. Effort is required not only because we need to overcome habits of inertia and selfishness, but also because a central feature of our lives is our free will. For love to be integrated into our heart, mind, and character, our love must also pass through this fundamental aspect of our being: our will. We must experience ourselves intending to love, choosing to love. Then we experience ourselves as becoming more loving.

Sometimes only a faint intention is required to give, sometimes a stronger intention is required. The night I gave Susan that massage, my appreciation for how much she gives in her life allowed me to give with relative ease. As I walked into the kitchen and saw the stack of dishes, a greater intention was required to overcome my inertia. Yet in both cases, once I was in the experience of giving, love took over my intention.

As important as intention is, it is not everything. Love gives through us. Normally, we should first direct our intention to reconnect with our love; then we can intend to give. Giving is an interplay of intention and opening ourselves to love, which then flows through us into action. Intention opens the dam so that the river of love may flow. Once that river of feeling is flowing, intention can stand by and enjoy the scenery.

Sometimes, however, it seems that intention is everything. This is especially true when the obstacle to our love and giving is a strong attachment, or when we are in a habit of inertia when it comes to giving. A few years ago, I had an experience that showed me an area of my life where I had to exercise great intention in order to free my love.

For several weeks I had been preoccupied with work and had not been spending much time with my family. One day at work I became acutely aware of this, and I resolved to give more attention to Susan and our two girls. When I got home that night, I immediately went into the kitchen where Susan was preparing dinner and began to help her. After dinner, I spent some time helping our oldest daughter with her homework. When we finished that, we talked about some of her trials with friends at school. Then I read a few stories to our youngest daughter, and we wrestled. The evening could not have been going better. Then something happened that changed everything: I glanced at the TV schedule.

Although I am not a hardcore TV addict, I definitely had a weakness for watching old movies on TV. As I scanned the schedule that night, my eyes were greeted by a sight I could hardly believe: My all-time favorite Italian western was coming on in a few minutes. This was the best, most "spiritual" western ever to come out of Italy, or any country for that matter. Because it was one of Sergio Leone's more obscure works, it rarely aired, and then usually after midnight. Only a couple of people I had ever talked to had even seen it. I had been so blessed in my life to have already seen it three times.

Excitedly, I told Susan the news (I had dragged her to see this movie with me a few years before). She made a face, "Oh, that again. I thought we could take a nice walk together as a family."

"No way!" I said with unrestrained glee.

Well, the rest of that evening I not only failed to give, but I was irritable and impatient with anyone who walked into the room to interrupt my watching. I even saw how I was acting at the time, but I couldn't help myself. I was totally possessed by my attachment to that movie. My irritation and impatience with everyone else managed to completely reverse the effects of any love I had given previously. While I sat glued to the tube, Susan and the girls went to bed feeling I had neglected them. I had.

Sometimes we disconnect from our love simply because we are attached to something else. Maybe it is a hobby, a favorite sport, the TV, or the newspaper. We all have many subtle attachments. When these attachments become habitual, they virtually become addictions. We don't see them as such only because we so rarely try to overcome them. When we do try to pull ourselves away from them—not just to partake in another attachment or tend to an obligation, but to do something constructive that is not required (such as giving to each other)—then we feel the powerful pull of these subtle addictions. Often, without knowing it, we put our attachments ahead of our relationship, our children, not to mention our own happiness and growth.

It is ironic that we invest so much of ourselves in the subconscious hope of finding our happiness in a love relationship, but when it comes down to it, we often fail to *consciously* invest ourselves in that hope. That is, we may put so many things ahead of the relationship—careers, golf, friends, TV, computer games—how, then, will we ever fulfill the promise of the heart? We won't. It is that simple. There is no way it can happen without our full desire.

The growth of love requires the greatest conscious investment of ourselves. We must feel a deep desire to walk this path. If we put TV ahead of our relationship, we can only partially experience the joy of a loving relationship. If our partner also likes TV, we may at least sit next to each other for a few hours a day. But will we learn to love fully, unconditionally? It simply won't happen. Our desire to master the art of loving is not yet strong enough. The promise of the heart will elude us. We are still too caught up in the habit of serving our own desires to allow ourselves to be an instrument of love.

Again, a relationship challenges us in the most personal ways. To fully receive each other, we need to be open in our hearts to each other. We cannot be preoccupied, driven, addicted to other things. We need to be able to drop other concerns when we are together, to put each other first. A love relationship challenges us to live in a balanced, fully present way. This requires a growth of self-mastery. We must gradually become self-possessed, freed from our subtle addictions. Only from a state of freedom do we gain the ability to give with any consistency. Only by a combination of will and grace do we gradually gain this freedom.

Most spiritual traditions of the world extol a certain degree of self-denial. In our society, however, we do not widely recognize value in self-denial. We like to give full sway to our individual freedom to pursue our own happiness. Yet this freedom can easily result in an imprisonment by habitual attachment and personal imbalance.

Just as giving integrates love into our lives, exercising self-discipline to free ourselves from our habitual attachments integrates strength into our lives. This strength is invaluable in overcoming obstacles to achieve both our material and spiritual goals in life. On the path of love, it is invaluable in overcoming the inertia that may keep us from growing. Yet there is no sense in self-denial for its own sake. Repression never works. Once we clearly see how we are addicted, however, and how our attachments are depriving us of the happiness and love we really want, self-denial is not denial at all, but a giving of life back to ourselves.

In *The Art of Loving,* Erich Fromm writes:

> *It is essential, however, that discipline should not be practiced like a rule imposed on oneself from the outside, but that it becomes an expression of one's own will; that it is felt as pleasant, and that one slowly accustoms oneself to a kind of behavior which one would eventually miss, if one stopped practicing it.*

If you feel that inertia is keeping you from giving, try to focus on giving just two things a day to your partner. Such an effort is specific enough that it will certainly not involve repression—only some intention. Just two acts of giving a day, above and beyond the call of duty, can work wonders in a relationship.

As simple and superficial as this might seem, this exercise requires a new awareness. It breaks our patterns of inaction and opens us to love as a dynamic, living experience. It means asking yourself: "What can I do to give? How can I serve the happiness of my partner?" It means noticing your partner's life; noticing the state of cleanliness of your home; noticing whether your partner needs help with something, like cleaning the kitchen, or weeding the garden; noticing the emotional needs of your partner. Does he or she need your support, your help? Even a hug, a kiss, holding hands, or simply offering to spend some time alone together can be an expression of giving.

Not least of all, it means noticing one's own habitual laziness when it comes to giving. It means resisting that laziness. For the sake of a job (often one we aren't crazy about anyway), we can force ourselves out of bed in the morning; why can't we, for the sake of our love and our own personal fulfillment, force ourselves out of habitual nongiving unconsciousness? Our life together is a gift, the most precious gift we have. We can waste this gift, living in the inertia of selfishness, or we can live with an awareness of the preciousness of this time we have together.

This raises an interesting point: When we give, we do not *give up* anything. We gain exactly what we are looking for: a blissful, expansive experience of love. Yet giving is only possible within the appearance that we do sacrifice something. The appearance of sacrifice must remain, for we cannot give out of selfishness.

It is fascinating to see that life has created this possibility of being recreated by love through giving, by painstakingly evolving the apparent need for just the opposite: taking care of ourselves first.

Thanks to the evolution of our physical bodies, we experience pleasure and pain, comfort and discomfort, satisfaction and dissatisfaction. These physical sensations call upon us to take care of ourselves. The reality of our physical separateness, that our nerve cells do not extend into each other's bodies, calls upon us to take care of ourselves *first,* ahead of the needs and desires of others. This is reality at the obvious physical level of our existence.

The more identified we are with the apparent boundaries of our bodies—our separation from the rest of the universe—the less sense giving makes. The more we feel defined by this separateness, the more rigidly entrenched we will be in a sense of "I" and "mine." This sense is only too familiar to the selfish individual ("my life, my rights, my money, my car, my food") who claims possession to all that relates to their survival, comfort, or pleasure. Subconscious identification with our separateness is the root of our resistance to giving. It is at the root of ideas of fairness and equality. The more one is bound by separateness, the more the survival of the fittest makes sense. Giving will rub against the grain.

With a little further evolution of consciousness, we may see the value of cooperation for the sake of our mutual physical survival/comfort. Mutual giving and receiving does make sense, even in terms of our personal survival, comfort, and pleasure. The existence of society is an expression of this evolution. The vast majority of modern love relationships are an expression of the principle of cooperation—mutual fulfillment of desire—on a personal scale.

Yet just as many threads of selfishness persist within society, so these persist in an intimate relationship where mutual benefit, and thus fairness, is a concern. When our personal desires for happiness are frustrated within such a relationship, we react. If it happens enough, we may even split up. One need only sit in divorce court for a while to see that such love can readily turn into its opposite—hate. At this level of evolution, we are still bound by our fundamental sense of separateness.

To give freely, as an expression of love, implies that the well-being of others is as important as our own. When we give, we love others as we love ourselves. Such love overcomes the sense of isolation, of separateness from others. It is the basis of true intimacy. Giving is a triumph of spirit—love, which unites us with others—over matter, which appears as a field of separateness, of duality and thus of fear.

Giving is a twist that completes billions of years of evolution. It is the twist that turns the instinctive desire for comfort, security, and pleasure inside out; then fulfills that desire by recreating life in the unity and wholeness of love.

CHAPTER SIX

THE PATH OF BLISS

Transforming Desire into Love

*O*f all the shared experiences the path of love can bring, perhaps none is more mysteriously, exquisitely beautiful and fulfilling than sexual union. Making love can spark the most tender feelings of appreciation, intimacy, and bonding. Most couples looking back on their relationship would find that many of their highest and deepest experiences together have taken place during lovemaking.

This is a great paradox: Love is more than sex, yet the passion, vitality, and creative feeling in a relationship arises from the chemistry between the sexes. We are sexual beings; to be human is to be either *man* or *woman.* Just as the mystery of human life and growth is contained within the DNA of the sperm and ovum, the mystery of realizing the promise of the heart is in large part contained within our sexuality.

This is not to say, however, that the secret to a fulfilling relationship lies simply in basking in the joys of uninhibited sexual pleasure. I have counseled couples who maintained they had a great sex life, yet suffered a miserable relationship. As with every other aspect of an intimate relationship, to be fulfilled, our sexuality must gradually be recreated by love.

When we first fall in love, sex may possess an almost magical power to unite us in heart, mind, body, and soul. Passion, attraction, appreciation, sexual desire—all at a peak—combine to create a fresh, blissfully fulfilling sexual experience. At no other time do we so deliciously feel the relationship between our body and our feelings. To open our bodies to each other is to open our hearts to each other in the most exquisite, delicate, sensuous vulnerability and love. The power and beauty of this experience not only fulfills sexual desire, but even our hearts' deepest longings for union.

Yet, for every couple, this graced state eventually changes. As we live through the challenges of intimacy, the trials of differing attitudes, expectations, and ways of doing things, the fresh bloom of romance fades and a subtle and gradual transition in the sexual relationship begins.

At first, we may hardly notice this transition. Even though the magic of romance fades in other areas of the relationship, for most of us, the sex drive continues; and for many, the sheer pleasure and physical intimacy of sex is enough to keep the magic alive in the bedroom. Yet this in itself hints at the change that takes place: Sex becomes more a fulfilling of sexual desire than the fulfilling of our hearts' longing for a union of love. Instead of *opening* ourselves to each other, we are doing something together.

In a brief or casual relationship, sex as recreation may bring all the fulfillment we could possibly want. Even in a long-term committed relationship, such sex may satisfy for months or even years; but gradually, the glow will wear off. Maybe we begin to feel that our partner does not love us "for ourselves," or maybe we feel just some vague sense of being let down after sex; maybe we would like to feel more tenderness during sex, or more caring and intimacy outside the bedroom. In a long-term relationship, we need to feel more than sexual pleasure. We need to feel the mysterious, fulfilling richness of our hearts opening and touching.

To the extent sex becomes recreational, it cannot fulfill that desire. Since the *end* of recreational sex—physical pleasure—is already known, we become to each other a *means* instead of an end. Sex becomes subtly impersonal. We have sex, we may even have what some might think of as great sex, and yet a lack of intimacy creeps in. We do not feel the wonderful closeness and richness of feeling that sex once stimulated.

Many couples wistfully recall the passion and romance of sex in the early days of their relationship, and attempt to recapture that passion. Rather than advance on the path of love, they put all their energies into regressing.

They may explore new positions, spice up foreplay, and experiment with new forms of stimulation. This often revitalizes a relationship for a while—just as taking up an exciting new sport together might—but in time this new sport, too, will fail to satisfy.

Our bodies are not separate from our feelings. To unite our bodies without uniting in our hearts with an equal intimacy violates the wholeness of our being. If it's recreation we're after, we would be better off taking up skiing. As Fulton Sheen put it, "The separation of soul and body is death. Those who separate sex and spirit are rehearsing for death."

We can communicate more; but if we do not communicate with more love, it will not improve our relationship. We may give more; but if we do so without feeling, it will fail to bring us closer. We may improve the mechanics of sex, and not improve the relationship at all. In recreational sex, no matter how stimulating, we are not loving each other; we love our own desire through each other.

A couple of years ago, at a relationship workshop I offered, a man in his mid-thirties approached me for advice. He described how the sexual attraction he had once felt for his wife had seemingly vanished. For years they had a great sex life; now, she was just the same old familiar face. In fact, he saw only her flaws. He was at a loss to explain this turn-off, for everything else in their relationship seemed fine. He was also concerned that he was feeling strong attraction to other women.

Swings in attraction and a roaming eye are common hazards of recreational sex. From turn-on to turn-off; from tantalizing, seductive beauty to familiarity. In recreational sex we don't love each other as we really are; we see only a reflection of our own desire. This may be flattering in the heat of sexual passion—to feel that one is tantalizing and seductive—but it can backfire once our desire is spent, when our partner loses interest.

Reality is different in different states of feeling. To see each other as we are, and to feel fulfilled within our relationship, we must see with the eyes of love. We must fully receive each other; and this is as true of receiving each other's bodies as it is of receiving each other's personalities. Within a person's eyes, skin, lips, breasts, arms, chest, breathes their character, their uniqueness and beauty as a person. This subtle beauty, which is a reflection of the beauty of the whole person, can be accurately appreciated only by the serene subjectivity of mature love. Then, even our partner's physical imperfections will seem to hold their own beauty, in that they are part of the person we love.

Following recreational sex, our interest may wane, for our attraction was based on desire that has now been satisfied. Following loving sex, we still feel our appreciation and attraction, for in loving sex we embrace the inexhaustible beauty, depths, and mystery of each other's personality. Sexual desire thus becomes a catalyst for enlivening a richness of feeling that is blissfully fulfilling, in each and every moment. The secret of finding sexual fulfillment is to find the fulfillment of love in sex.

TRANSFORMING DESIRE INTO LOVE

*L*oving sex may sound good, but what do we do when, despite our good intentions, all we really crave is some good old sexual satisfaction? The human sex drive does not always cooperate with our intentions to be sensitive, tender, caring, or even "normal." The path of love holds many challenges, and not the least of these is to discover how passion can deepen our love.

The maturing of our ability to love involves an almost infinite number of minute steps: of inner healing, of gaining insight and self-knowledge, of opening to our feelings and to the feelings of others, of growing in selflessness and inner freedom. We must take each step as it arises organically. If we strain, if we attempt to forcibly skip a step, we will leave some corner of ourselves in the shadows of unconsciousness. It is sure to come back to haunt us, by undermining our ability to feel, give, and receive love. The first requirement for growth is to be where we are: located in our true feelings, desires, and needs. When we are aligned with ourselves, with our own nature, then our nature can evolve.

Yet there is one qualifier to this requirement: In being where we are, we must be *in the totality* of where we are. We need not repress feelings, needs, and desires; but to heal and grow, we do need to experience these within their underlying context.

For instance, when I am in conflict with Susan, communicating is unlikely to create communion unless I connect with the feelings underlying my immediate reactions. I need to open to the pain, insecurity, and love that underlie my anger. When I do that, even bitter conflict can lead to a rich connection with my partner. How much more potential for a rich communion of feeling must exist within sexual desire! Yet unless we connect with all the layers of our feelings, even sex will not guarantee intimacy.

When amorous, I am primarily aware of my desire for sex. If I simply act on that desire—approach my partner, show affection, engage in foreplay, have sex—I pursue what to some degree is an impersonal, recreational approach to sex. I use my partner to fulfill my desire. In the process, we may also experience a connection in our hearts, but by no means is this guaranteed. That is not even my primary intention. My primary intention is to fulfill myself sexually.

There are, however, many other feelings that form the hidden context of my sexual desire. Connecting with these is the key to conscious, loving sex. It is the key to using sexual passion to accelerate the growth and maturing of our ability to love, to becoming more whole.

If, instead of engaging my partner without a thought as to what I am feeling, I were to pause and be quiet and mindful of myself for a moment, I might first discover within my passion my desire for love, companionship, and closeness. This desire exists within every heart. If I consciously connect with *this* desire, act to fulfill this desire, then I vastly increase the probability that we will experience the fulfillment of love in sex.

In exploring beneath my sexual desire, I may also become aware of other feelings: residual tension from the day, wanting to escape from some outside pressure or stress, wanting to forget some uneasy inner feeling, say of sadness or insecurity. Jumping into recreational sex, I may feel relief from inner or outer stress in my life, or I may not. I may temporarily escape from my concerns, only to later spend a restless night tossing and turning with them. If I connect with my desire for intimacy and love, open to my partner, feel a connection in our hearts, the result will be much more healing. The intimacy of loving sex is much more nurturing and healing than the isolated gratification of recreational sex.

Loving sex also creates an ideal atmosphere for healing sexual problems—one of safety, trust, respect, acceptance, and a lack of expectations and demands. Loving sex heals by dissolving the anxiety, insensitivity, and emotional isolation that can accompany recreational sex.

The opportunity to channel passion into a deepened experience of love, then, begins with the inception of sexual desire, long before we are in bed together. Every amorous impulse can be a reminder to connect, not only with our attraction for each other, but with our appreciation and caring. Every amorous impulse is a reminder of our desire to feel our intimacy. Thus it is a reminder to express our love verbally and nonverbally, to give attention, support, or help, or to simply spend time together. Sexual desire then passes through love. It becomes less driven, for it awakens the fulfillment of love. At the same time, the more attentive and appreciative we are toward each other, the more we feel our attraction. We naturally begin to feel the desire to be as close and intimate as possible; we may feel like we want to climb inside of each other—only this desire is coming from our love.

In this way sexual passion is recreated by love. Our desire is no longer impersonal and purely physical, but personal and centered in our hearts. Our desire comes into a more natural perspective within our whole being. This desire for union need not always express itself in making love, but when the chemistry is right for both partners, it will, and the result will be a delicious union of love.

This points up a basic difference between recreational sex and loving sex: The more love we feel, the more fulfillment we receive from simply loving each other. Loving sex is the play of this fulfillment. This is far removed from recreational sex, in which couples enter the bedroom with any number of desires and expectations. In recreational sex everything from the inception of sexual desire, to getting each other into the mood, to foreplay, to intercourse, to climax, to dropping off to sleep afterward, is motivated and conditioned by specific desires and expectations, most of which have little to do with love. For this reason, loving sex bears little resemblance to recreational sex. In fact, loving sex requires forgetting everything we normally do leading up to, during, and after recreational sex.

The first thing we can forget in loving sex is getting each other into the mood. The need to get each other in the mood only arises in recreational sex; driven by desire disassociated from love, we jump over creating a communion of love, and instead try to create a *communion of desire*. We unwittingly treat our partner as an object with which to fulfill our desire, whereas when we are fully connected in our love, we are together in our feelings and desires. We are naturally drawn toward greater intimacy and union. One does not have to manipulate the other to fulfill their desire.

If, however, one person is in the mood and the other isn't, and there is a true communion of love, then that is something to talk about and explore. That is a situation ripe for growth, insight, and healing. If we remain open and loving, something significant will come of it. We will learn something about ourselves. We will move toward healing whatever hidden attachments, fears, or pain stands in the way of our unified desire.

Next, we can forget the usual preoccupations of recreational sex; for instance, fulfilling specific erotic desires, having an unforgettable orgasm, climaxing together. We can be innocent. We can hold each other, look into each others' eyes, verbally express our appreciation, share our thoughts and feelings. We can enjoy being together as two whole persons in love. Throughout our lovemaking we can maintain a loving connection. Sex is a catalyst to deepen our love; it need not replace our love.

Loving sex means noticing where our passion is leading us. Is it leading us into more love? Or is it leading toward an impersonal experience of sex? Are we feeling more and more connected in our hearts? Or are we becoming absorbed in getting and giving pleasure? In recreational sex, we focus our passion on body parts. In loving sex, we direct our passion toward each other as whole people, while we enjoy the natural pleasure of making love. If we find love falling into the background, we can slow down. We can talk, express our love, hold each other in a way not specifically designed to give sexual pleasure. We can give connecting in our hearts a chance. With just a little effort, the wildly erotic can often settle into a much richer and more satisfying communion of feeling. Then we may continue to make love, connected in our hearts.

Sometimes this will be easy. At other times it will require discrimination, self-discipline, and a deep desire to become more loving. Only by consciously diverting desire into love do we take love in sex out of the realm of chance. Love, even during sex, must become, as Scott Peck says in *The Road Less Traveled,* "an act of will—namely, both an intention and an action." We need to consciously attend to our love, even during lovemaking.

This may appear to take the fun out of sex, but nothing is more sublimely fulfilling than lovemaking as a union of love. The aesthetics of self-gratification hardly compare with the aesthetics of making love. Loving sex holds infinitely greater richness, depth, and nuances of feeling. Love is inextricably bound with beauty; the more love, the more beautiful, the more fascinating, deeply uniting, and fulfilling the sex.

When we are focused only on our love for each other, we are fully connected with each other. We feel each other intimately. We may even feel every nuance of each other's thoughts, sensations, and emotions. For this reason, we can also forget another preoccupation of recreational sex: the how-to mechanics of sex.

In loving sex we usually will not have to be told what to do or how to do it. We need to focus on the mechanics of giving each other pleasure, either because we are absorbed in our own pleasure, or because we feel pressured to fulfill expectations—our partner's or our own. When we are simply loving each other, neither do we make demands nor feel pressured. We are not trying to live up to any image, or to fulfill expectations. In connecting with our love, we allow each other and ourselves to connect with our natural ability as superb lovers. If at any point one needs to guide the other, giving that guidance in the context of loving sex will be much easier, and it is much more likely to be willingly received.

Finally, in loving sex we can forget about the major preoccupation of recreational sex: orgasm. When sex is a gratification of sexual desire, we can hardly help but anticipate an orgasm. Everything we do moves us in that direction, even though to prolong pleasure, we may take detours. All that we do in recreational sex leads to that one event, and this anticipation itself is a hotbed of potential problems. It draws our attention to the mechanics of sex. When we focus on mechanics and body parts rather than on the whole person, we are unlikely to feel as deeply personal a connection. Further, if one person regularly climaxes before the other, it can create resentment, even lead to insecurity regarding one's ability to perform, or about sex in general.

In loving sex we are focused only on loving each other. The more we are focused on our love for each other, the less we are focused on orgasm. In *Love and Will,* Rollo May makes this distinction in terms of sex and eros: "It can be agreed that the aim of the sex act in its zoological and physiological sense is indeed the orgasm. But the aim of eros is not: eros seeks union with the other person in delight and passion, and the procreating of new dimensions of experience which broaden and deepen the being of both persons." This is the essence of loving sex.

When we make love with no expectation of orgasm, focusing only on connecting intimately in our hearts as two whole human beings, then each and every moment of lovemaking is blissfully fulfilling. Whereas orgasm once provided the greatest pleasure, this deep, personal, touching of hearts becomes most fulfilling. As a result, couples can be entirely fulfilled sexually—with or without an orgasm. (This includes both men and women.) Thus, there is no underlying agitation of anticipating an orgasm.

Nevertheless, a couple may find they have more ecstatic orgasms than ever, but spontaneously, without making this the focus of their lovemaking. They may surprise themselves by experiencing everything they always wanted in sex. They may also find at times that they feel so filled with their love, that an orgasm would be entirely beside the point. A couple's focus on love may also result in supersensuous orgasm-like experiences that do not entail physical orgasm—what one sex expert terms "psychasms."* These releases of blissful, loving sensuality are every bit as fulfilling as the best physical orgasms, and both partners can experience many in a single episode of lovemaking.

As a result of a loving focus and the lack of concern with orgasm, couples may also find that loving sex lasts much longer than recreational sex. We can bask in our love for hours without the slightest strain. This, however, only happens naturally when both partners are entirely focused on love. When making love, we are highly sensitive to each other. We can literally feel each other's feelings and thoughts. If one partner is obsessed with achieving an orgasm, this will often draw the other partner into the same goal, and the pace of lovemaking will quickly become that of recreational sex. In any case, how long sex lasts is not important. Loving sex is just that: loving sex. It is not a technique of prolonging recreational sex.

*Paul Pearsall, Ph.D., director of the Problems of Daily Living Clinic, Department of Psychiatry, Sinai Hospital of Detroit. Author of *Super Marital Sex* (New York: Ballantine Books, 1987).

Though loving sex can open whole new vistas of sexual pleasure, such experiences are not the measure of its success. In fact, the moment a couple makes any particular experience the goal of sex, the moment a couple even anticipates any particular sexual experience, they have strayed from loving sex. Loving sex means only one thing: passion deepening our experience of intimacy and love. If this happens, then whether or not we rise to new heights of sexual ecstasy, our lovemaking has been brilliantly successful.

Gradually, we become more discriminating as to which acts during sex detract from, and which acts deepen the connection of our hearts. We discover that what were once ultimate turn-on's are far from satisfying—because they distract from the luxuriant supersensuality of loving sex. Recently, one husband who had come to me for counseling volunteered the following description of how his marriage evolved from recreational sex into loving sex:

> *My wife and I used to be really into erotica. We made love in just about every conceivable position and then some. Not that we couldn't stop ourselves, we* didn't *want to stop ourselves. Then my wife was in a serious auto accident and the shock of almost losing her left me, left both of us, more serious about our relationship. It also changed the quality of our sex. We began to stay with each other during sex. Sometimes we would revert to just getting it on, but when we did we both noticed that we didn't experience as much feeling for*

each other. Somehow, just going for the gold didn't even seem as enjoyable as it used to. We actually felt kind of let down. Not that we felt guilty or ashamed— we weren't sexually hung up or anything. It was more like how you'd feel on a game show when you realize you chose the curtain with the set of steak knives instead of the curtain with the brand new Camaro. We just both knew deep down that we had missed out on something.

Anyway, a lot of the things I used to love to have her do for me I didn't even like anymore. And she didn't like to do them anymore either. It was like we both grew up. Now when we have sex, we just make love, and we're really connected in our hearts, but it feels better than our private orgies ever did.

This couple had to experience for themselves the difference between stimulating organs and stimulating love. They stumbled onto the only way anyone matures in their love: their desire evolved organically.

Though this evolution involved trial and error, they did not simply have recreational sex until they got sick of it. Instead, the wife's near death connected them with their desire for intimacy and love. As they acted to fulfill this desire, they discovered that loving sex was *better* sex. As a result, old habits of recreational sex became less appealing. This organic preference for loving sex over recreational sex, felt not just intellectually, but in their whole being, was a mark of their deepening as individuals. They had become a little wiser, a little more capable of intimacy, of mature, conscious love.

Neither can we force ourselves to prefer loving sex. We can only stay in touch with all our desires, innocently giving preference, without repression or straining, to those we know will lead us in the direction of love. We can only follow the charm of increasing love with sensitivity, giving, and innocence. Our deepening will come about gradually, naturally, through experience.

Yet even experience will remain impotent to produce this deepening without a deep desire and intention to master the art of loving. A couple may remain at more or less the same level of sexual experience for their whole lives, without ever having the least hint of how to grow and deepen love through their sexual relationship—because they have no idea of what they are missing. Only the desire and intention for something more lets us know when we have settled for something less.

With this desire for more, even if all we feel is good old carnal craving, we will still grow through our experience. We do not need to deny or ignore our sexual appetites. We need only surround them—innocently, without straining—with our desire to grow in love. In other words, we simply keep in touch with what our lives together are about—even during sex. We may still end up slipping into recreational sex, but at least we will have set ourselves up to receive the feedback on having done so. We will be much more open to experiencing not just shame or guilt, but the pain that recreational sex entails.

It may seem puzzling to speak of sex as painful, yet recreational sex is invisibly permeated with pain. Recreational sex deprives us of a rich experience of intimacy, caring, and tenderness. It expresses only one isolated aspect of our desire; it reinforces the divisions within ourselves. Habitual recreational sex not only deprives us of feeling genuine caring and intimacy, but gradually makes these appear unattainable ideals. Suppressing our hopelessness of ever experiencing a deep bond of love, the desire to grow in love withers. As a result of all this, the relationship becomes less attractive. To anyone at all in touch with themselves, this degeneration is indeed extremely painful.

By connecting with our desire to mature and deepen on this path of love, we connect with ourselves as whole persons. The light of personal meaning illumines our experience. The brighter this light becomes, the more clearly we see the shadows it casts—we feel the pain of separation from ourselves and our love. Whereas we once may have thrived on recreational sex, we are now impatient for the depths of love.

Yet this impatience need not bring guilt or shame. Growing is a natural process, not a matter of morality. Trial and error are inevitable on this path. There is no reason to feel prolonged shame; we can simply feel the pain and let the pain pass. If we feel pain over an action, let us learn from that pain. We can see at what point we turned from love. We never have a better chance to gain self-knowledge than when we are still smarting from the pain of an action. If that pain spurs us to bring more love into our lovemaking, then it will have served us well.

OPENING OUR HEARTS TO EACH OTHER IN LOVE

*F*inding our own desire for love is one thing, but what happens when one partner wants an intimate, loving connection, and the other partner just wants some good old erotic recreation? One wants tenderness, and the other wants sexual gymnastics. One wants to feel loved, and the other wants to feel thrills. Such discrepancies in sexual desire can result in plenty of resentment and alienation.

If both partners have expressed a preference for loving sex, then it should not be necessary for one to forego a personal connection in order to fulfill the recreational desire of the other. For example, if my partner wants erotic recreation, it is not only a matter of sexual desire, but that she is disconnected from her love. If I wish to help my partner reconnect with her love, then above all else, I need to remain loving. Resisting or criticizing will not help. Teaching or explaining will not help. Without refusing my partner, I can gently, inconspicuously lead us toward the charm of love. I can ask about her day, make eye contact, show some appreciation and nonsexual affection. If I stay in my heart, I can draw my partner into her heart.

We need to learn to help each other find our love in this way, not only as a preface to sex, but at other times as well. We are on this path together; all of us lose touch with our love. There is no cause to become impatient or irritated, because the situation could easily be reversed tomorrow, next week, or the next hour.

Nevertheless, it is not always easy to break out of old patterns. I once counseled a couple who genuinely desired a more loving connection. Yet, as the wife complained, she could not even hug her husband without him making sexual innuendoes. He also wanted to break out of these patterns, but found it surprisingly difficult.

Growth requires the energy, attention, and courage to let go of familiar habits and experiences that may have been a part of our lives and relationships for years. Though breaking any habit can be difficult, habits in the arena of sex can be particularly resistant to change—the attachment to old pleasures runs deep. One especially effective aid to breaking old patterns of recreational sex is to periodically call a "sex fast." A period of conscious, loving abstinence from sex can "reset" a couple's sexual relationship.

TAKING A BREAK FROM SEX

*M*y wife and I have found sex fasts to be an important part of our growth right from the beginning of our relationship. Initially, we observed sex fasts because we noticed that in satisfying our sexual desires, we might feel fulfilled for a day or two, but then we'd feel just as much or even more craving. At times, sex seemed a spiraling attachment that didn't have a whole lot to do with love. Simply fasting from sex for a week or more helped break patterns of attachment so we could start fresh and hopefully connect more in our hearts. Later, we began to realize that we could also use our period of abstinence to focus on loving each other in other ways. This greatly amplified the value of our sex fasts in terms of letting us feel a fresh intimacy and caring for each other. Eventually, we found sex fasts invaluable for other reasons, which will become clear later.

During a sex fast, then, we abstain, not simply for the sake of breaking old patterns, but also to redirect our attraction into other expressions of love. We do not want to simply cultivate freedom from old patterns, we want to cultivate love. Thus, rather than simply abstaining from sex, we can put all our attention on connecting in our hearts through showing affection, giving, and verbal expressions of our caring. As a result, we begin to discover for ourselves that our love can be independent of sexual desire. We discover that we are capable of giving love freely.

How long a sex fast lasts is entirely up to the couple. For some couples, three days is an appropriate fast; for others, two weeks is better; and some may wish to fast longer. How long a sex fast lasts is not important; how well we use that time to connect in our hearts is what counts—as well as then bringing that loving connection into our sex life once we break our fast.

As with breaking any kind of fast, it is best to come off a sex fast gradually. We do not break a food fast with a feast; we do not come off a sex fast by jumping back into old habits of lovemaking. Newfound sensibilities will be delicate. We should take the time to enjoy this delicacy. Following a food fast, we may savor even the simplest foods. After even a one-day fast, a baked potato can taste ambrosial. Foods once gulped down without a thought become sumptuous delights. In breaking a sex fast sensitively, we enjoy the simple nourishment of being together, touching, holding; loving each other as whole people brings exquisite satisfaction. Thus, a sex fast can be a new beginning of a more loving relationship. We need only let the newfound delicacy of our love guide us.

Over time, the benefits of a sex fast may gradually fade. This is natural. Nevertheless, we have gained a new touchstone. We know what it means to consciously channel our attraction into nonsexual expressions of love. We know loving sex in our own experience. We know that a loving relationship is not a myth, an impossible dream. When we feel the need to, we can again observe a sex fast. When undertaken in this spirit, sex fasts can be fresh beginnings in the growth of a more heart-centered relationship.

Sex fasts have another, more esoteric significance. Emotional healing, which involves actual shifts in the functioning of the mind, emotions, and body, requires energy. Thus deep emotional healing happens much more readily in a restful state, such as during meditation or contemplative prayer. Sex, and to a lesser degree the enjoyment of any sensual experience, expends energy, both subtle and obvious. It dissipates the energies needed to focus in the subtle areas of our being where healing profoundly opens our hearts and our consciousness, not only to each other, but to life, to God. This is not to imply that anyone should forego all sensual enjoyments, but rather that growth and healing require that we live with a degree of discipline, so that we have enough energy and power of inward focus to heal. Living a balanced life, we can both enjoy life, and heal to the point where our hearts are open in love to every being in creation.

The mystical and esoteric teachings of the great spiritual traditions of the world have long recognized the spiritual power and depth that can develop when continence is combined with regular spiritual practices such as meditation, devotion, and prayer. Sex fasts are a form of continence that allow us to restore subtle energies necessary to our growth and healing, necessary to the opening of our hearts. These energies also nourish subtle aspects of the body, enhancing health, intelligence, creativity, and well-being.

Nevertheless, as wonderful as the benefits of continence are, growth must still be natural and organic. We should not extend sex fasts to the point where we feel strained or dry in our hearts. No spiritual tradition of the world recognizes continence alone as a viable means of spiritual progress. Rather, we must combine continence with spiritual practices that cultivate qualities of the heart; then sexual energy is transmuted into spiritual energy—into love.

Merely conserving sexual energy, without developing love, is of little benefit. Thus, in a sex fast, we do not merely abstain, we focus on expressing love in other ways. This may be considered one "spiritual practice" that transforms the energies we conserve into love. Naturally, if we also engage in traditional spiritual practices like meditation and prayer, we will further magnify the value of a sex fast.

Occasionally, a couple that is seriously dedicated to their spiritual growth will raise the question whether or not they should consider celibacy. Complete celibacy is appropriate only if a couple finds that their love is deepened by their abstinence, not diminished. In that case, it will be what both partners organically desire. In other words, we needn't ask anyone this question; we follow the charm of love. Love, after all, is the goal of spirituality, not dry asceticism. Even if one person deeply desires celibacy, if their partner does not, then a mutually agreed upon balance of loving sex and sex fasts is infinitely preferable to forcing their partner into repression—or into an affair.

Over the years I have met a number of couples who confided in me that they were completely celibate for spiritual reasons. Unfortunately, this decision often proved premature. I have seen some of these couples suffer prolonged emotional dryness, affairs, and even divorce. Yet I also personally know several celibate couples who report exceptionally fulfilling relationships, as well as tremendous acceleration in the growth of their inner spiritual experience. It is interesting to note that in each of these latter cases, the decision to remain celibate was hardly a decision at all, but a preference that developed organically, after years of marriage and deep devotion to a spiritual path.

For most couples, however, an intimate relationship that enhances all of the dimensions of love described in this book, including loving sex and mutually agreed upon sex fasts, approximates what celibacy and selfless service are for a monk or nun; both lifestyles convert sexual energy into spiritual energy, sexual energy into love. (Because loving sex is often fulfilling without an orgasm, when this happens loving sex itself becomes a lesser form of continence. Loving sex combined with sex fasts may also serve as a natural form of birth control.) When we open our hearts to each other in love, we melt the boundaries that keep us isolated from each other, ourselves, and God. Love coursing through us heals and expands us as nothing else can. We need simply, innocently, follow the charm of love, with discrimination and discipline, remaining open to discovering the next level of our growth.

Sex fasts are essential for any couple truly interested in maturing in their love. Couples who find themselves making love night after night are falling into a pattern of recreational sex, whether they know it or not. The path of love is an adventure into new territory, not an endless repetition. As love grows, we come to see that our desire for sexual union is actually the physical expression of a deeper urge toward a union of love. If this urge is always channeled into a physical sexual expression, our love will not mature. Our sexual desire will remain compulsive and impersonal. Our urge toward union must be allowed to breathe life into our whole personality. The growth of love means we become more whole.

ABSORBING EACH OTHER THROUGH LOVE

As we become more whole, we will find our lives and our relationship becoming naturally balanced. We will find that we enjoy being together in many ways. We will find that we can *make love* and experience the richness of love much more of the time. That is, our ability to make love becomes independent of sex. We begin to feel a consistency of love in our relationship, a maturity of love independent of any particular act or any particular pleasure. This love is a much more sumptuous, giving love. Our hearts open to each other in a tender, exquisite vulnerability and love, in and out of sex. Romance returns to the relationship, only now it is more conscious, mature, and a sign of our own deepening as human beings.

This growth happens as we fully absorb each other through our love. Earlier, we discussed balancing and uniting the masculine and feminine poles within the personality through receiving each other. Nowhere does this happen more powerfully than in loving sex. Here, in our naked intimacy, we are potentially most vulnerable, most open to receiving each other. Here our intimacy can melt the boundaries of otherness—within our relationship with each other and within our own hearts. Here, our love unites the sexual poles within the personalities of both partners.

This cannot take place in recreational sex, however, for recreational sex depends on the perception of our sexual partner as wholly *extrinsic* to us. In recreational sex the object of desire must remain just that: an object—a thing characterized by otherness. In recreational sex we may be physically intimate, but we are psychically polarized. Not only does this dominant perception of otherness preclude true intimacy with one's partner, it also precludes the possibility of uniting the masculine and feminine poles within oneself.

The experience of true intimacy begins as impersonal sexual desire is tempered by personal love. Through love we experience the true beauty of each other. We are drawn to each other, we receive each other, we absorb each other; polarities dissolve. Rather than focusing on body parts and an outward flow of energy through orgasm, we receive each other through our hearts. We drink each other in, we merge with each other, and so with the opposite sexual pole within ourselves.

In this growth of wholeness together, we experience the meaning and beauty of male and female. At one time, the feminine qualities of the woman may seem so rich, springing from a source of beauty so deep, that they seem to surpass the beauty of the masculine qualities within the man. At other times, the reverse will seem true. We may each be humbled by the beauty of the other. Both man and woman contain infinite richness and beauty. In different cultures and in different times God has been conceived as both Male and Female: God the Father, and Mother Divine. The couple growing on the path of love discovers the truth of both conceptions of God. Through our love, we come to hold both within ourselves.

CHAPTER SEVEN

UNION

The Three-Dimensional Relationship

*T*he American writer Henry Miller once wrote, "In expanding the field of knowledge we but increase the horizon of ignorance." This applies not only to knowledge, but to love as well.

As we walk this path, we will not only have many reassuring experiences of deepening love, closeness, appreciation, tenderness, and caring, but we will also inevitably become aware of the imperfections within our love. Most of us will find that long after we have embarked on this path together, there will still be times of conflict, times when we feel separate, when we see each other's faults more clearly than each other's beauty, times when we can't communicate or don't want to communicate, times when we feel no inspiration to give, perhaps even times of wondering if we'd be better off apart. These times too are a part of our path together.

Yet what of the promise of the heart, the path of love? We may tell ourselves that the journey is the destination, that we are only human, that we cannot rightly expect to be perfect in love. All true. Still, the more the light of love shines in our lives, not only the more fulfillment we feel, but the more we may yearn for our perfection. This too is only natural. Indeed, as we have seen, our intention to excel in the art of love is vital. Otherwise, we are bound to settle for less than what we are capable of. Who is to say what that is? Yet nothing I have described so far will bring us that perfection. If this were all there was to know about love, the full promise of the heart would ever be one step beyond our reach.

Up to this point, we have discussed love in two-dimensional terms: love for each other, love for self; healing each other, healing self; communicating with each other, communicating with self; receiving each other, the growth of self. This two-dimensional view of love has one great limitation: We act as if our love is based on ourselves. We, however, have our shortcomings; sometimes we are just plain not loving, sometimes we are just plain not lovable.

So long as our love is based on ourselves and each other, our mutual shortcomings provide the seeds of reaction. So long as my partner can behave selfishly, the selfishness within me can react. So long as my partner can reject me, I can react and reject my partner. So long as our love is based in each other, we can never master the art of loving. We will have times when we deeply love each other, but we will also be subject to fluctuations in our ability to receive, to feel our love, to give. No two-dimensional relationship is entirely secure, no matter how hard we work at receiving, communicating, inner healing, and all the rest. We need to focus on all of these aspects of our relationship, but to live the promise of the heart, we need more. We need to anchor our love in a third dimension.

A couple of years ago, I had a profound personal awakening of this third dimension of love in my own life. At that time I was editing and designing a book, *The Way of Marriage,* which I intended to publish myself (Harper-Collins later bought the rights). I had carefully worked out a calendar of deadlines as to what had to be done in order to get the book to distributors and especially to key pre-publication reviewers in time for the book's release. Without these key reviews, the prospects that a book will succeed are seriously handicapped. As the weeks passed, and my deadline for sending the book to press approached, I realized that I had vastly underestimated the time I needed to edit and design the book.

I had spent the better part of two years writing the book. The thought that its success would be undermined now was discouraging, to say the least. I decided that I had to meet my deadline, no matter what it took. I talked to Susan about it and she agreed; I would put all other work on hold and for three weeks go all out to finish the book.

For those three weeks I worked an average of fourteen hours a day, seven days a week. I worked during meals. I took only one short ten-minute break during the day for a walk. I slept five hours a night at most. My focus was total and intense. The only part of my normal daily routine that I preserved was my time spent in meditation and prayer. For many years I had spent several hours a day in prayer and meditation; as far as I was concerned, nothing was important enough to sacrifice that time, but now I cut even that by a third, and got up at 5:00 A.M. to do it.

Much to my surprise, far from wasting me, this grueling intensity seemed to open some invisible floodgates of grace. My creativity and clarity soared. Whereas I had been feeling grouchy before, practically going into a panic whenever the kids or Susan interrupted me, now I felt calm and collected. If the kids interrupted me, I responded to them with patience, took care of them, then went back to work. Yet the most amazing effect of this intensity was on my prayer life.

For years my meditations had steadily grown in richness, but now, literally the moment I closed my eyes, I tangibly felt God's presence. As I continued in either prayer or meditation, I would experience intense feelings of devotion, while my mind became so concentrated in the experience of God that at times I would seem to dissolve altogether into the infinity of God.

There is no describing this infinity of God into which all thought, feeling, experience, and even one's sense of selfhood altogether disappears, but I can give an analogy. Imagine that you are the sun. Imagine that in addition to indescribable energy and light, your being similarly consisted of qualities of love, intelligence, and joy. You are thus a vast ocean of pure intelligence, light, love, energy, and bliss. Yet there would be a limitation to your being as the sun: At some point, you end and space begins. So, say you were a billion suns—a billion-times-vaster ocean of pure intelligence, light, love, energy, and bliss. Still, there would be a limitation to your being. Somewhere, you would end. The experience of the infinity of God is like this, only there is no limitation. Never does that ocean end. A billion billion suns would be a drop in that infinity. Yet in that ocean of God, there is not one single stirring—not one single wave, not a single impulse of thought. Absolute, infinite peace and silence.

Now, forget that analogy: The infinity of God is beyond that and beyond all qualities whatsoever. These qualities increase to the point of infinity as one approaches God, then achieving infinity, they cease to be. The moment one again gains individual awareness, one knows only that one has experienced God: infinite love, intelligence, energy, bliss, peace, silence.

Regaining individual awareness, the indescribable divinity of God's personality—the most delectable, sweet, pure, Divine Love—filled my heart. To some degree, this feeling would last throughout the day, and it seemed that God was in some invisible way taking part in all my actions. I had never before felt so much an instrument, nor so much grace.

I make no claims to any degree of spiritual attainment. Far from it. My family will gladly testify that I am no saint. On a path involving contemplative prayer and meditation, with consistent and long-term practice one may gradually develop the capacity to experience God in varying depth and clarity. This is invaluable to one's spiritual progress and to perfecting love. Thus I urge anyone on this path to daily spend time in meditation and prayer. Yet the greatest challenge is integrating this experience into one's daily life, into one's personality, thoughts, feelings, and actions. Sure enough, this is just the challenge that arose for me that week.

Between my total, one-pointed focus on readying my book for publication, and the rapturous experiences of meditation and prayer, I had hardly given a thought to Susan. Neither had I kept up with my usual chores. After all, she knew how hard I was working and why, and that it would only last a few weeks. She had agreed that I should do it. Nevertheless, I began to notice a tension building. When I would say good night, she would respond without enthusiasm or would just complain about something. During the day, when we passed each other, she seemed distinctly grumpy. I tried to talk with her, but I kept getting a minimal or grouchy response.

Finally, I realized that this called for special measures. I decided to take an evening off and take Susan out to dinner, just the two of us. We did go out together, but the evening did not have the desired result. Susan admitted she was feeling a lot of anger, that she could not feel her love for me, but she refused to tell me what was bothering her. She said it wouldn't help to tell me, that she had to work this out within herself. I pleaded that she tell me, so we could talk it out as we always had, but she remained firm.

I believe this was a first in our entire relationship. In the past, at worse we would communicate our grievances only too well. This silence seemed far more hurtful than an argument; I felt entirely shut out and alienated from her. I wondered if our relationship was in some jeopardy of which I was unaware—and on the eve of publishing a book on marriage. What a great theme that would make on the talk show circuit: "My marriage was going great until I published a book on it!"

The next morning I woke up early, as usual. After meditating, I went downstairs and prepared breakfast. I still felt irked that Susan was imposing such a boundary between us. As I prepared breakfast, I did some mental gymnastics in an effort to receive her, or to at least understand her. I failed miserably. Not only was she reacting to me, but she had shut me out, and I could not muster a single impulse of love for her.

I said a silent prayer asking what I should do about it. The answer came to me in a second. I had been feeling such grace, yet I had not applied it in my relationship with Susan at all. Thinking that I had only to get my book published, I had even fallen back into old habits of letting her take care of the household.

With that thought, I noticed that the dirty dishes and pans from the kids' dinner last night were still sitting on the shelf. This was another first in our relationship; Susan had never in all our years together allowed dirty dishes to remain overnight. In that moment, to me, those dirty dishes seemed to shimmer with grace. Clearly, they were meant for me—maybe by Susan, but certainly by God; at least they were a good starting place. Just the thought of doing them filled me with love. I dove into the task.

Though my heart had softened toward Susan, I cannot say that I was feeling my usual love for her. Nevertheless, I was filled with love. The love I felt was love for God, or rather, it was God's love in me. Within a few moments of starting the dishes, however, my heart also opened to Susan, until I did feel my love for her, but *within* my love for God. After finishing the dishes, I looked for something else I could do. I swept the floor and fixed the attachment to the water purifier (which had been spraying any hapless user for a week). These few actions seemed the blissful beginning to what I intended to be many more. Finally, I went to work on the book.

A little while later, Susan woke up and I heard her downstairs. Still feeling a tenderness for her, I went downstairs, and gave her a hug, which she returned rather lifelessly. I asked her how she was feeling. "I've got a cold," she said in a nasal tone. "Are you going to need the car today? Because I do," she added a bit coolly.

"No, I don't need it," I replied. Her tone was like a bit of acid dropped on my bliss. Still, I felt compassion for her. "Well, I hope you feel better," I said, giving her another hug, and then went into my office to work.

Within a few minutes, my office door opened and Susan stood in the doorway. "I really appreciated your vibration of caring and support downstairs," she said with genuine feeling. Her face was much softer. "And I did notice the things you did. Thanks."

I got up from my desk, walked over to her, and again we hugged, for a long time. This time she returned the hug.

For the next few weeks, Susan still seemed to be going through some ragged feelings, but she was no longer holding me responsible. Instead, she continued to express her appreciation of my support and caring. Though she was experiencing some emotional purification, we were together, feeling intimate and caring. What she was going through even allowed us to experience our closeness all the more. For my part, I knew that I had not only come to a new level of inner spiritual experience, but my love had stepped to a new level of freedom. (This story in no way characterizes the balance of love in our relationship. There is no question that Susan is more developed in her love than I. Indeed, I write from my own experience, in part because I tend to exemplify many of the common obstacles to love. When I take a step on this path, it is a source of wonderment for all who know me, myself included. Hopefully this will encourage others.)

In our relationship with each other, we stand as imperfect equals. In our inner relationship with God, we stand in relation to the infinite perfection of love. We dissolve in the equation. As we dissolve, we can surrender so much more, give so much more, recognize with humility our own challenges so much more than in simply our relationship with each other. As we dissolve, the limitations to our love dissolve. (As St. John of the Cross expressed, "To arrive at being all, desire to be nothing.") Standing in relation to each other, we feel resistance to allowing ourselves to dissolve. Standing in relation to God, we delight in dissolving, for then we can become what we love; we can become Love. Then our love for each other becomes a reflection of Divine Love.

Thus the fullness of love is more than a feeling, it is a state of being. The more you become Love, the more you simply love. Your love is not restricted to your partner, nor to family and friends, but extends even to those who may dislike you. When you are Love, you love all. As Christ enjoined,

> *Love your enemies and pray for those who persecute you; in this way you will be sons of your Father in heaven, for he causes his sun to rise on bad men as well as good, and his rain to fall on honest and dishonest men alike. For if you love those who love you, what right have you to claim any credit? Even the tax collectors do as much, do they not? And if you save your greetings for your brothers, are you doing anything exceptional? Even the pagans do as much, do they not? You must therefore be perfect just as your heavenly Father is perfect.*

(MATTHEW 5:44–48)

Unfortunately, most interpret this to mean that such unconditional love is primarily an act of will. Certainly, intention and will play a role in the growth of love, but the state of being Love is not sustained by will. Rather, it is sustained by the experience of Divine Love. This experience is gained not merely by an intention to imitate God's love, but by loving God so intensely—with all one's heart and mind—that one's heart and mind melt into God; then we become one with God's Love. Only then may we love all as the sun shines upon all. Only then do we live the full promise of the heart.

You may wonder, if this is the secret to living the promise of the heart, why have I bothered to discuss at such length the details of a two-dimensional relationship? Why did I not make this the first chapter in the book, and skip all the rest? This is precisely the reason why. We would be tempted to skip over all the details of our lives, to forget about the intricately meaningful moment-to-moment challenges necessary to our ripening in love. We would want to live the state of being Love simply by repeated acts of will, and that will never work. Our ideals would remain just that: ideals.

We can no more grow in our love through a one-dimensional relationship than in a two-dimensional relationship. The desire and intention to love God, without that love showing itself in every moment and every circumstance of our lives, is a one-dimensional expression of love. It is not even as compelling, rich, or real as two-dimensional love (love for one's partner) can be. In a day and age when we suffer the embarrassment of even religious leaders scandalizing themselves, this point cannot be missed. Love is not fully Love until it is three-dimensional, until it embraces all of our life. Spiritual life is fully integrated life. Love only becomes Love when we feel the reality that every circumstance of our lives, every moment is a gift of deeply personal Love for us.

This is why we must attend to the details of our lives. As we open ourselves to experiencing personal meaning within our challenges—especially challenges that arise in our relationships with loved ones, for these are our most direct challenges to love—we make one of life's most remarkable discoveries: *Personal meaning exists.* We do not have to create it. It is intrinsic within every circumstance of our lives. Gradually, this discovery goes deeper than our intellect, and finds its way into our heart. We *feel* the reality that within our experience are hidden opportunities to deepen, to find the center of ourselves, to heal, to unfold our love and giving. As we feel ourselves deepening, learning to love, feeling the joy that comes with healing and growth, our heart begins to open to that mysterious, vast source of grace and meaning within our lives. We cannot but begin to feel a deep gratitude and love for God.

It is here, within this inner personal relationship with God as an immediate experience within our lives, that the third dimension of love—Love—becomes real. We cannot melt in love for God until we fully feel God's personal Love for us, as we appreciate the gifts of Love we are given in each moment. Simone Weil said it well: "Love of God is pure when joy and suffering inspire an equal degree of gratitude." Love cannot become Love except by embracing the whole range of life.

As we embrace the wholeness of our lives—our sufferings as well as our joy—we come into the center of ourselves. There, in our center, we find that a precious flame of love has ignited, and once ignited, it must rise higher. It can only rise, for this flame is grace itself; it is the grace of the growing perception that everything in our lives is a gift, and such grace can only bring more grace.

Still, if our love is to become pure, we must endure times of pain and purging. As our personal limitations to love melt, the pain, fear, and insecurity that previously held those limitations in place are released. Susan's ragged feelings during that period were such an experience of purification.

Thus, part of growing together is learning to support each other not only in our togetherness, but also in our inner journeys. We need to not only give each other space, but to listen and nurture with understanding and compassion. Whereas I could not do this from within my relationship with Susan, it became nearly effortless from within my relationship with God. In a three-dimensional relationship, even in times of pain, we can support each other unconditionally. Even in solitude, we can walk the path of love together.

We can also better see the meaning of times of pain and purging. We can watch the clouds of purification come and go. We need not let dark suggestions of failure take root in our hearts. With faith those clouds will pass all the more easily. With faith we may see that all we go through together purifies our spirit and our love. Every argument, conflict, and hurt becomes a purging of the obstacles to love within us; every experience of deepening intimacy and joy is a ray of the flame of Love gradually being revealed in our hearts. Faith reveals this flame of Love, which, rising, frees us *and* binds us in a fathomless union of shared experience and feeling. In this sacred fire of love we live the promise of the heart.